W9-BQY-192

In token of Christian love,

Simon Blocker.

# The Secret of Pulpit Power

# THE SECRET OF
# PULPIT POWER

## THROUGH THEMATIC CHRISTIAN PREACHING

by **SIMON BLOCKER, D.D.**

*Professor of Practical Theology*
*Western Theological Seminary*
*Holland, Michigan*

**WM. B. EERDMANS PUBLISHING COMPANY**

**Grand Rapids**      1951      **Michigan**

# Table of Contents

PREFACE ........................................................................... 9

## PART ONE

THEMATIC CHRISTIAN PREACHING ................. 11

    I. What Is Thematic Christian Preaching? ................. 13
    II. How to Get a Good Theme for a Sermon ............. 22
    III. How to Scale Thematic Heights ............................... 31
    IV. Thematic Searchlights on Sermon Structure ........ 40
    V. Structural Aspects of Thematic Sermons ............. 50
    VI. Surplus Values of Theme Construction ................. 56
    VII. The Birth of a Thematic Sermon ............................ 65
    VIII. Selection in Thematic Sermon Construction ........ 76
    IX. Thematic Expository Preaching ............................... 86
    X. Thematic Topical Preaching — Usual Form ........ 95
    XI. Thematic Topical Preaching — Special Form ...... 104
    XII. Thematic Textual Preaching ................................... 113
    XIII. Thematic Doctrinal Preaching ............................... 122
    XIV. Thematic Narrative Preaching ............................... 131
    XV. Thematic Sermon Delivery ..................................... 142

## PART TWO

DEMONSTRATION SERMONS ................................... 147

    XVI. A Thematic Expository Sermon:
            Christian Security ..................................... 149
    XVII. A Thematic Topical Sermon —- Usual Form:
            The Fire of Jesus Christ ............................ 158
    XVIII. A Thematic Topical Sermon — Special Form:
            Christian Certainties ................................. 167
    XIX. A Thematic Textual Sermon:
            Christ and World Crisis ........................... 178
    XX. A Thematic Doctrinal Sermon:
            Does the Church Matter? ......................... 190
    XXI. A Thematic Narrative Sermon:
            Good News for Sinners ............................. 202

# Preface

This book is written for the Christian ministry as well as for students for the ministry and lay preachers. Christians generally, who are interested in Bible study and who would welcome a fresh way of getting at the heart of a Bible passage, can profit by it. The thematic quest in sermon preparation can become a thrilling adventure in spiritual discovery.

No book in the field of preaching known to the author covers the same ground as this one and the method of presentation is in part different also. Principles of sermon construction and types of sermons are illustratively discussed in terms of actual Bible texts or passages. Six sermons are given in full of as many types of sermons, not because they are perfect models, but because they are such as average preachers can be expected to produce from week to week. Constructive criticism of these sermons by students and preachers may serve to accentuate the principles of sermon construction presented.

The author has served twenty-eight years as pastor and preacher and fifteen years as professor of preaching, including the preaching opportunities such a position includes. Over forty years of experience have impressed many matters herein shared.

The state of the world faces the Christian preacher with almost unparalleled challenge. Now as always, the Christian preacher must show that he has what the world needs and that he is paying the price of putting it over. The Christian ministry should appeal to the most brilliant minds when it so imperatively needs in its ranks the equivalent of the best leadership in other spheres of human interest and activity.

It is believed that those who master this book will increase their competence as preachers and by God's grace experience a real uplift in their work as ambassadors of Jesus Christ.

SIMON BLOCKER

# PART ONE

# THEMATIC CHRISTIAN PREACHING

# I

# What Is Thematic Christian Preaching?

THEMATIC Christian preaching is the proclamation in sermonic form of God's self-revelation as contained in the
Bible. When a man preaches, what he preaches is called a sermon. It may not merit the name "sermon." It may not be
charged with the substance of God's self-revelation as recorded
in the Bible. If it contains the redemptive truth of Biblical
revelation, it may not be organized into true sermonic form.
It may be a running commentary, or like an article in a religious encyclopedia, or just a number of thoughts. It may
be sermonic in substance but not in form, or sermonic in form
and not in substance. Preaching is big business and a properly
constructed sermon is its effective form. To organize the truth
of a verse or passage of Scripture according to the specifications for ideal sermon structure is to implement it as the
sword of the Spirit of God.

A thematic Christian sermon does not necessarily or inevitably contain all the truth taught by a verse or passage of
Scripture. A Bible verse or passage may contain two or more
truths of primary importance or one primary truth and one or
more subordinate truths. To preach thematically calls for
appraisal, grading, selection and classification. Major stress
is wisely laid on acquiring and preaching the primary meaning, especially by students for the ministry and young clergy-
men. Experience is a wise guide in directing proper use of
the secondary and the subordinate aspects of the primary.

The term "thematic Christian preaching" covers both substance and form of preaching and has very special significance in view of current religious confusion. Consider, first,
the substance of thematic Christan preaching. Thematic

Christian preaching is a highly specialized scientific technique for proclaiming glad tidings from God, the good news of God's redeeming grace in Christ. Christian preaching is the proclamation of a Divine crusade of redemption, of God's way out of our human predicament. What God has done to make possible true self-realization and true self-expression is recorded in the Bible and constitutes the substance of genuine Christian preaching. God has made Himself available in Jesus Christ to meet the totality of human need.

Thematic Christian preaching proclaims God's offered deliverance from moral guilt, moral defilement and moral impotence. It promises Divine relief from frustration and despair. It heralds God's cure for fear, doubt, ignorance, self-idolatry, triviality, futility, and every conceivable threat to decent, well-ordered, radiant, vital living. It reveals the secret and source of divinely integrated personality. It is the declared manifesto of the supernatural and ideal social order made possible, practicable and imperative by God's grace in Christ. It announces and makes real, eternal vistas and horizons, showing God's eternal future through redemption for a doomed and dying humanity. The matter of the substance of thematic Christian preaching could properly take us far in an effort to express the total significance of God's self-revelation in the Bible. God's speech and action are unspeakably meaningful and the Bible is unspeakably wonderful as the record of God's speech and action for human salvation.

Thematic Christian preaching is thus primarily concerned with what the Bible says and means from the standpoint of its main Divine intention. The Bible is always to be regarded as the record of God's self-revelation, as a history of God's introduction of His kingdom among men, as the story of a Divine crusade of redemption, as an inspired account of the moral order of the universe; of God's character and saving interest in a lost world, of the person and work of Christ, of a door of hope and a way of salvation for mortals hard beset by the folly of unbelief and sin. The Bible was never intended to be a battleground and storm-center of schismatic conflict.

It is God's Guidebook for erring stricken mankind, telling man what to believe and what to do, with the dynamite of God in it to beget, increase and empower faith and the necessary dynamic also to produce Christian character and personality and a Christian social order.

Thematic Christian preaching stresses Biblical content as well as sermon organization and structure. The content of Christian preaching must serve the total significance of Biblical revelation. A verse or passage of Scripture is to be interpreted in the light of its context. It is absolutely necessary for a Christian preacher to master the contents of the Bible, to know what is in the Bible, book by book, to engage in constant, persistent, unremitting Bible study, to accompany industrious searching of the Scriptures with earnest, believing prayer for the illumination of the Holy Spirit, to continue to ask God to grant ever new experiences of the power of the Word of God, to make daily supplication for the perpetuation of the joy of salvation and for grace and strength to do the known will of God, all in order that the preacher's life may become saturated with the regenerating truth of God. The truth of God is creative of Christlike atmosphere, of Christian disposition, of supernatural insight, of spiritual realization and of a passion for souls. These undergird, buttress and make mighty thematic Christian sermons. No use talking about form in Christian preaching if the Christian preacher does not have substance of Biblical revelation and Divine redemption in his own soul as a personal, realized, rapturous experience.

In considering the substance or content of thematic Christian preaching, it has been shown that such preaching makes imperative, first, a constantly growing knowledge of the Bible in its total, that is to say, redemptive significance; secondly, repeated personal experience of the power of the Word of God; and thirdly, a realized personal salvation kept constantly up-to-date by faithful use of the means of grace. It remains to show, fourthly, how thematic Christian preaching, if sound in redemptive content, tends more and more to lift the preacher and thus also a congregation out of and above the atmosphere of controversy.

If a Christian preacher is willing to sweat blood to become a mighty prophet of God, let him study and master how the apostle Paul dealt with the controversies which raged in the church at Corinth. It will suffice for the purpose to study Paul's First Epistle to the Corinthians. He will discover the strange cause of contentions among God's people. He will learn that these arise as the result of blind spots induced by arrogance and pride. Whence come pride and arrogance among God's people? The answer is startling. The Corinthian Christians had such a rushing tide of spiritual life and such an abundance of spiritual gifts that they were led to admire the gifts and their possessors instead of keeping their eyes on God the Giver of these gifts of grace. With sight focussed on diversities of gifts among the leaders, they began to develop and express preferences. This introduced schism, contention, partisanship, and blind-eyed bickering. Full soon, a great church, a group of wonderful Christians, divinely endowed with rare spiritual gifts, begins to take sides, call names, deprecate certain leaders, developing blind-spots to the total significance of God at work in Christ to achieve a full salvation, so much so that some even denied the resurrection of the dead.

Let every present and prospective preacher get and keep in mind how Paul dealt with the situation. Paul lifts the gaze of these Corinthian Christians straight up to God, straight up to God in Christ. The church at Corinth is shown to be the Church of God. Its existence is due to the will of God. The reason there are Christians and a church in Corinth is the grace of God incarnate in Jesus Christ. Paul stresses "the word of the Cross" and "God's good pleasure through the foolishness of the preaching to save them that believe." Christians are sternly and lovingly made aware of the church's one foundation. "We preach Christ crucified, Christ the power of God and the wisdom of God." The Divine source of redemption and the supernatural character of the Christian life are emphasized and magnified with overwhelming force. "But of God are ye in Christ Jesus, who was made unto us wisdom from God, and righteousness, and sanctification and redemption: that according as it is written, 'He that glorieth, let him glory in the Lord.'"

The cure for controversy among Christians and the pride out of which it springs is concentration on the grace of God that brought salvation, God's operative grace in Jesus Christ. If the atmosphere of the Christian life and the Christian church are to be Christlike, the thought-life of individual Christians and of churches must be Christ-centered. It is indeed astonishing that Christians, lifted so high by God's grace in Christ, can fall so low and from such an eminence. Such is the peril of not keeping one's gaze fixed on Christ. The Christian life and the Christian church and Christian gifts and endowments of every kind are all of grace and are all ours in Christ. But God must have the glory and Christ must have the preeminence if there is not to be a crash into the sordid atmosphere of controversy.

Consider, therefore, in view of this Divine disclosure of how it is among God's people, the vast importance of thematic Christian preaching, the substance of which gives God the glory and exalts Jesus Christ. How important it is that the Christian preacher pays the price of being qualified physically, intellectually, emotionally, morally, spiritually, dynamically to preach the whole counsel of God, to lift God's people to the proper levels of Christian thinking and feeling, to keep the life of the church in an atmosphere of Christian unity, possible only by ever increasing sensitiveness to the glory of God and the grace of Christ the Saviour.

Apart from the matter of controversy and divisions among Christians, so productive of tragic strife and of lost power in the Church, reflect on the control in wide areas of Christian life of the secular, the trivial, the selfish, the sensuous. The Christian life cannot be the wonderful life God means it to be and Christ makes it possible to be, unless the wonder of salvation through God's grace in Christ remains a live, sensitive, operative consciousness in Christians. This wonder of a Divine salvation for us who do not deserve it can only be kept fresh by the means Divinely ordained, by habits of personal Christian living and constant hearing of thematic Christian sermons by preachers who know that their Redeemer lives, who are masters of the truth of God's Word, who come to fresh visions and revelations of the Lord as renewed experiences of the power of the Word of God reward their prayerful study of it, in whom the joy of salvation is like a rushing river, who glory in the Cross of Christ and make their boast in God.

Consider, now, the technical form of thematic Christian preaching. A thematic Christian sermon expresses its essential spiritual message in a single sentence at the close of a brief introduction. The rest of the sermon, called the body of the sermon, is the development according to specific principles of that one Christian truth or idea. The single sentence which embodies the leading thought of the sermon is called the theme of the sermon. It states a proposition, enshrines a truth, conveys a warning, sounds an alarm, presents an inducement, proclaims deliverance, administers comfort, reveals an insight, makes a prediction, offers pardon, peace and power, all in harmony with God's redemptive purpose in Christ and each as Bible verse or passage requires.

The theme is drawn from the Bible verse or passage which is the basis of the sermon and expresses its abiding, universal, contemporary, redemptive significance. The theme must be short and simple enough to be clearly understood and easily remembered. It must be as strong and dynamic as possible. Though simple, short and strong, the theme of a Christian sermon should be comprehensive enough to suggest either directly or by implication the necessary development of the theme in the body of the sermon.

The preacher may choose two or three or even four lines of thought to develop his theme. These lines of thought must be aspects of the truth of the theme. They are usually called the divisions of the sermon. Each division is to be clearly stated at the beginning of its development. As an aid to clarity of thought and to facilitate remembrance by both preacher and listener, the divisions are announced first rhetorically and then logically. To state a division rhetorically is to put it in the form of a subject or topic. To state a division logically is to put it in the form of a sentence. Each division is thus introduced by a statement in topic form of its line of thought, followed by a sentence containing a fuller disclosure of the aspect of the theme to be developed.

The purpose of the introduction of a sermon is to present the theme and the proposed lines of its development. This latter is best done by stating the divisions rhetorically. A further purpose of the introduction is to enlist the interest of the congregation. The first sentence of the introduction has thus been regarded as of unusual importance. It has been called "the attack upon the text" and more recently "the approach to the sermon." It must be striking and it must arrest attention.

The theme of a Christian sermon should be stated in universal, timeless, terms if possible. By this is meant that the names of specific Bible characters are not put into a theme. The same holds true of Bible events. The exception is that the Father, the Son, and the Holy Spirit, the one true God is always in place in a theme whether as subject or object. This holds for Bible events which express God's saving action in history. It is surprising how hard it is to keep the human out of the subject of the sentence which is your theme, and how easy it is to keep God or Christ in a subordinate place. A preacher will often have to come to a definite showdown in this matter. A safeguard is to remember Jesus Christ at all times and to labor to give Christ the preeminence in sermon themes as well as in sermons. The formal discussion of sermon theme thus far will be further described and fully illustrated in a separate chapter.

The conclusion of a sermon follows the body of a sermon and answers the question, "So what?" The unfolding of the theme in the body of a sermon reaches its climax in the final division or line of thought. The conclusion appraises the value of the truth of the theme which has been developed in the divisions. Thus it is that the conclusion of a sermon is often spoken of as the application. The conclusion may summarize the truth presented, indicate its practical bearing on human needs and interests, stress the urgency of decision and committal and set life where it belongs in the presence of the Cross of Christ and the light of eternity.

Thematic Christian preaching can only be the technique of a truly redeemed man. It is the channel of the power of God. In this type of preaching only God is great. The preacher is charged with what Paul calls the testimony of Christ (I Cor. 1:6). Vast supernatural powers are operative in preaching that merits the descriptive term "thematic Christian preaching." These are such as the power of the Word of God, the power of the Holy Spirit, the power of the grace of God, the power of the blood of Christ, the power of the resurrection of Christ, the power of faith, the power of prayer, the power of a surrendered life. There is no ground for praising a preacher when he meets the requirements of His Divine vocation. "May Jesus Christ be praised!" Hunger for compliments shuts off the powers mentioned. Preaching for praise may be successful in getting praise. What more, then, does a preacher want? It is as if God said to such an one: "You got what you wanted; you have your reward."

How wonderful are Paul's words! Keep them near as a standard of measurement. "And I, brethren, when I came unto you, came not with excellency of speech or of wisdom, proclaiming to you the testimony of God. For I determined not to know anything among you, save Jesus Christ, and him crucified. And I was with you in weakness, and in fear, and in much trembling. And my speech and my preaching were not in persuasive words of wisdom, but in demonstration of the Spirit and of power: that your faith should not stand in the wisdom of men, but in the power of God." Here surely is the secret of great preaching. It takes Pauline weakness and fear and trembling to clear the way for "the demonstration of the Spirit and of power." Says Karl Barth, "An impressive apostle as such would be no apostle. A winsome testimony would as such be no Christian testimony." It must be insisted concerning the Christian pulpit "that no flesh should glory before God." It is where there is an end of man's wisdom and greatness, that, as Barth says, "the Christly begins, the testimony of Christ the crucified on the side of the speaker, and the faith which is not man's wisdom but God's power on the part of the listener." What a channel of supernatural forces a Christian preacher and pulpit can be when self is on the cross and Christ on the throne, when the thematic Christian preacher knows by personal spiritual experience and proclaims "what is sent us from God in Christ the crucified!" Barth is a true interpreter of First Corinthians when he maintains that "all speaking and listening in the Christian Church is based upon the assumption of the divine, holy Spirit, which opens here the mouth, there the ears."

# II

# How to Get a Good Theme for a Sermon

EFFICIENCY in determining and constructing the right theme for a sermon is the result of general and special preparation. It is not an inevitable product even of a regular course in a theological seminary. A student, about to graduate from a famous theological seminary, entered a nationally known religious book shop and asked if there were any books which would give him a knowledge of the contents of the Bible. He went on to say that the approach of his graduation made him aware of how little he really knew of what is in the Bible. Some books were mentioned to him bearing titles like the following: *Bible Study by Periods, Bible Study Book by Book, Bible Study by Doctrines, Outline Studies in the Old Testament, Outline Studies in the New Testament* and *Synthetic Bible Studies*. A purchase of some of these books was made, the student made work of it to master them and later said that a few weeks of industrious reading of these books had given him more knowledge of the contents of the Bible than three years of theological education. This reference is not intended as an aspersion on theological seminaries but shows that when a seminary offers over a hundred courses and makes many of them electives, a student may not have sense enough at the outset to elect first of all to master the contents of the Bible. He may possibly decide that he can master the contents of the Bible by himself after graduation and that it is imperative in seminary days to specialize in elective courses which may not be available to him after he is installed as pastor of a church.

To become a master in creating and constructing sermon themes requires a growing knowledge of the content of the

Bible, an ever deepening understanding of the meaning of Bible revelation and a fuller realization of its significance for personal life. If a student for the ministry is wise he will stoutly determine at the very outset to know his Bible. If the stress of work in Seminary days leads him to postpone large scale Bible reading until he enters the ministry, he will find that there are even more obstacles to mastering the Bible in a pastorate than there are in Seminary days.

A Seminary professor advised the members of an entering class to be sure to read the Bible through once during the three years of their training. One determined to do so and made up his mind to read ten chapters a day. He did not stick to it and when the class graduated, not one member had read the Bible through while in the Seminary. If the question could be asked of every clergyman, "Have you ever read the Bible through?" the answers might prove to be an astonishing disclosure.

A pastor who had just read a new book in the field of eschatology commended it to a minister friend and offered to lend it to him. The offer was accepted with hesitation, the friend explaining, "Eschatology means nothing to me." Three months later the owner of the book asked for its return and learned that his friend had not read it. The friend was one of that large number of ministers who could not understand why he did not rise higher in his profession. He was a genial man with a fine personality. Everything about him seemed to favor advancement but he was not a student of the Word nor of any other field of religious knowledge. His personality won him one fairly large church but in due time the church went "down" and the pastor went "out." His last charge was very small and he died in the full strength of years, not, as it seemed, because the vital energy of life was spent, but of a broken heart.

What the world needs is not a moratorium on preaching, but a revival of Biblical, Christ-centered, Spirit-empowered preaching by redeemed men who know their Bible. First hand knowledge of the Bible is the firm foundation on which a

preacher can erect a temple of truth which will draw humanity
to its holy light. This is but to say that the qualified Christian
preacher for such a time as this is one who is charged with
the power of the Word of God, who knows, lives, preaches and
radiates that Gospel of Christ which is the power of God unto
salvation.

The real redemptive substance of the Bible is even for many
preachers a vast unexplored continent. There is so much to
do, pressure is great, strength limited, Sundays recur so rapidly, that homiletic aids get priority and scissors and paste pots
rank as major implements in sermon construction. A minister discovered near the close of his summer vacation that he
had a growth developing on his chest. The physician advised
an immediate operation. The young preacher demurred, saying
that he was due back on the job very shortly. Then spoke the
physician, "Young man, you have no more important business
on hand right now than to attend to that growth." The clergyman submitted to an operation, the growth was cut out, sent
to a university medical laboratory for analysis, was found
non-malignant and the trouble did not recur. The immediate
removal saved the life. Is this not a parable of a sinister growth
in hard-pressed clergy, a growth away from the deep source
of a preacher's true message and power, a growth perhaps not
yet malignant in younger clergy, but a menace to the proper
functioning of a Christian minister, a growth of the pressure
of the subordinate, a growth which has killed the preacher in
many an older man of God. The whole set-up of a minister's
life today seems often to be such as to make it well-nigh impossible for him to qualify as a competent preacher and
prophet of God. Something has to be done about it. "The
King's business demands haste." One must act at once. Get
back to the Bible. Read it slowly but persistently. Take time
to do it prayerfully. Read it chapter by chapter and book by
book. Then study books on the Book that summarize contents
and give distilled essence, books bearing titles such as, *The
Living Messages of the Bible.* Thematic Christian preaching
is grounded on Bible knowledge and inspired by understand-

ing, appreciation and realization of its significance. The most solemn and drastic obligation rests on all preachers to master the Bible and be mastered by it.

In addition to studying the Bible for the purpose of mastering its contents, the thematic Christian preacher must specialize also in the devotional reading of the Bible with this question in mind, "What is God's message to me?" The danger of professionalism is very pronounced in the Christian ministry. Just as an undertaker is apt to lose reverence for the living human body because he is constantly handling the body when it has become a corpse, so a preacher's constant handling of sacred things may reduce them to lifeless forms unless he takes necessary precautions. When Christian doctrines become dead things to a preacher, he himself becomes "a dead one" as far as preaching is concerned. The preacher's devotional use of the Bible with accompanying prayer must be one of the priorities in a minister's daily schedule.

General preparation for thematic Christian preaching requires assiduous use of Bible commentaries. This means more than consulting commentators in loco on a specific verse or passage chosen for a sermon. A preacher must acquire the habit of reading commentaries on specific Bible books like a book-reviewer reads a novel. If you get a new commentary on a book of the Bible, read it through as soon as possible. Standard commentaries of a past generation may retain distinct values for after years and centuries, but no preacher can afford to neglect new, recent, up-to-date, modern Bible commentaries. We live in a new age of the world. Language changes. New conceptions give birth to new forms of expression. Commentaries by modern critical scholarship are abreast of the times. They speak in current tongues. Present-day preaching must be such that high-school and college students and farmers and plain folk can understand it. The personal Christian faith of the thematic Christian preacher must be strong enough to weather the gales of scientific Biblical criticism. Nothing permanent in vital Christianity has been outmoded by modern Biblical scholarship. Many of the greatest critical scholars of the Christian Church rejoice in Christ and His salvation. One who has the joy of salvation need not fear critical scientific Christian scholarship. To build up a solid background for thematic Christian preaching demands familiarity with the assured results of critical Christian scholarship. Only with such a background can a Christian preacher serve the present age. Sermon themes come more readily and are much more likely to be contemporaneously pertinent if the preacher who creates and constructs them is a scholar as well as a saint.

Further suggestions for general preparation for thematic Christian preaching must be made. Bible dictionaries, standard and new works in the fields of Systematic and Biblical Theology, and special books in the field of Christian doctrine, such for instance, as notable works on the Person and Work of Christ, must form the staple of a minister's reading if the treasure house of memory is to become a lying-in hospital for the birth of fine sermon themes. The preacher who schools himself to keep at school among master theologians and thinkers is sure to underwrite a development of power to think which will produce themes in twins, triplets and quintuplets.

Not every young clergyman may be aware of the value of Bible dictionaries for building up background for thematic Christian preaching. Take such a work as Hasting's *Dictionary of Christ and the Gospels.* Refer to the article by James Denney on "Preaching Christ." If that article were mastered and allowed to determine and direct the course of a Christian minister's pulpit ministry, it would revolutionize and regenerate wide areas of Christian preaching. One could look up with profit scores of verbs in such a dictionary after which the name of Christ would be most appropriate, such as "following Christ," "confessing Christ," "obeying Christ." What a course of sermons could grow out of habitual browsing in such a dictionary of Christ and the Gospels, what substance and quality of preaching!

The Christian preacher must major in works of the kind suggested to build background, lay foundations, sharpen convictions, determine trends, create atmosphere, keep cognizant of basic spiritual realities and to hew true to the line in the gigantic business of proclaiming the unsearchable riches of Christ. There is every reason to recommend classic books of devotion and the reading of sermonic literature. Vital as these are they are not as factually rich as the Christian preacher's task requires. They must be read for inspiration, for refreshment as to spiritual goals, for instruction perhaps in the art of simple, direct and beauteous expression, and as mirrors of the soul or balances in which appraisal of personal work is made. Yes, yes, read books, too, in the fields of religious education, Christian worship, church history, Christian evangelism, hymnology, Christian missions, Christian psychology, Christian sociology, Christian therapy, Christian psychiatry, and all areas pertinent to church administration and church programs and what have you. Every person who answers God's call to preach must become an inveterate reader of the Bible, of literature on the Bible and inspired by the Bible, of all books that promote the propagation of the Gospel and the building of the church. Read as if your life depended on it in order that you may be an authoritative apostle of Jesus Christ to a groping, sinning, struggling, disintegrating, suffering and dying race.

It is rewarding for a Christian preacher to read as extensively as possible in the fields of general culture, history, sociology, psychology, philosophy and science. The list is not at all inclusive enough. Great books there are in every generation that bear such titles as, *The Crisis of Our Age; God and Evil; The Problem of Pain; The Survival of Western Culture; The Way of Things; The Meaning of History.* It is necessary for a preacher to know the state of the world, to know the latest data on our human predicament, to understand the times in which he lives. If he reads a book of scientific facts written by a Christian called *Man Does Not Stand Alone* he will not forget to read the book of an unbeliever which produced it, bearing the title, *Man Stands Alone.* By scholarly excursions into many fields, yet giving the Bible priority in daily schedule, he constantly so increases his knowledge of facts and his store of wisdom, that he becomes an expert sermon themist, launching golden sentences which propagate the Christian faith and minister divine light and healing to minds diseased, as well as graded nourishment for the health and growth of Christian people.

Inasmuch as a thematic Christian preacher organizes his thought for a sermon into thematic sermonic form, he develops an eye for sentences in his reading which may serve as themes. It is easy to write the first letter of the word "theme" on the margin of a page opposite where such a golden sentence occurs. Every wise preacher accumulates as many sets of books as he can by the greatest variety of authors on such fields as the parables of Jesus, the miracles of Jesus, Bible characters and such like. The preacher who uses the thematic form of sermon structure develops an eye for themes as well as an ability to construct them himself. He becomes a more alert reader, a more vigilant scholar. Strange as it may seem, not every preacher has the ability to get the meat out of a book. A minister who decides to preach thematically, who, therefore, must have themes for next Sunday's sermons, cannot afford to be listless in study or careless in reading. He learns to linger over sentences, to ponder them to extract the essence, to take in the meaning. One of his favorite hymn lines is, "Sometimes a light surprises." He is apt to want to change it to read, "Full oft a light surprises." A Christian preacher can have real fun in the wonder-land of Christian truth. New light from God begets delight.

In answer to the question, "How to get a good theme for a sermon?" the answer is as indicated in this chapter. Acquire the art of constructing themes for sermons by mastery of the centralities of the Christian faith. Get great, standard old and new Christian books. Read them as if they were novels. As a basis for that, read, study, master the Bible and the aids to such study and mastery as the type of books mentioned makes possible. Pray without ceasing that God may set what you learn and know on fire, so that you may be a man on fire for God. Your special preparation will be the focusing of your general preparation on the particular Bible verse or passage to be expounded in your next sermon. Write your own themes. You can do it. You must do it. You mean to do it. You will do it. If in a pinch, special pressure is on you to borrow one from your reading, God bless you. But give credit and do not let it happen too often. Covet the joy of creating.

A series of expository sermons on some Bible book is a good way to add particular weekly preparation to general preparation. No series should be too long. A half dozen sermons ought to suffice. Put the pertinent commentaries and other relevant volumes right on your desk. Begin promptly on Tuesday morning to study them. Monday is the preacher's rest day. For a minister to work seven days a week is a sin of presumption. No minister can get away with it. Chickens come home to roost. Rest on Monday but start promptly on Tuesday morning the studious inspection of the ground for the next Lord's Day's sermons. No thematic Christian preacher can qualify with less than four hours of study a day. Any preacher who studies four hours a day is a growing man. Effects are cumulative. Begin on Tuesday morning your sermon preparation for the following Sunday. By Friday there will have been sufficient incubation to write themes, perhaps a hundred, before you strike the one that strikes fire. By Saturday you will wish it was Sunday so you could preach. Put the precious four hours of a morning in on your Bible, on commentaries, and Bible dictionaries. Work those four hours on sermons for immediate and future use. How are you to get four hours for study in the morning? The same way as farmers, factory workers and merchants. Keep pace with every man who goes forth to his labor. Get up in good time. How are you going to get ready for prayer meeting, Sunday School and other meetings requiring preparation of things to say? In time you will be rich in by-products of your basic morning studies. You will regularly gather up by the basketful the fragments that remain from your thematic sermons. Your fidelity to theme gives you a fund of glorious left-overs, grand ideas, brilliant flashes which can serve some future but not next Sunday's themes. You can use them in prayer meetings. But who taught you to preach in prayer meeting? Prayer meeting is the people's service of praise, prayer and testimony. The people must be encouraged to share Christian experiences. There is no authorization to turn a prayer meeting into a preaching service. It cannot go well with a church that loses its prayer meeting, or where lectures supersede prayer. A fragment or flash left over from last Sunday's sermons can strike the key and give your people the go-sign. Teach them, if necessary, one by one and in private, with yourself as the only public, to pray in public. Stick to your theme on Sunday and to your four hours of study per day from Tuesday until Saturday and you will build greater barns to store the mind's and soul's over-flow and from which to draw for other week day services. Now and then burn the barns because the scientific filing system can become a snare, but keep studying and praying and preaching thematically, dying daily, but finding out what it is to be raised with Christ and to live with Christ in the heavenlies. Follow this guidance and God's statutes will become songs in the house of your pilgrimage. In fact, be thou faithful unto death in this matter of thematic Christian preaching and of all that makes it possible and dynamic. Long before "unto death" gets any meaning other than the death of self unto resurrection in Christ, your themes will bid fair to become theme-songs. Themes come when you pay the price. They make sermons live. They come from God. You find them on highways of industry and prayer. Work for them. Pray for them. Preach them. Get them out of the Bible and so out of the heart of God. Base them on the Bible. Center them in Christ. "The light of the world is Jesus." You will shine with the reflected light of the Light of the world.

# III

## How to Scale Thematic Heights

Sermon structure is vital to effective Christian preaching. The best possible sermon structure is thematic. By this is meant that every sermon should have a theme, a fresh, crisp, brief, telling, succinct sentence containing the essence of the truth of a Bible verse or passage, contemporaneous in style and substance.

It is necessary to distinguish between the subject or topic of a sermon and the theme. Many preachers think that when they have a subject or topic, that the matter of a theme is settled. Topic and theme should be in harmony, but they are not the same. A minister advertised two subjects for his Sunday sermons. Morning, "Too Much Barn"; evening, "Too Much Kitchen." Another advertised the subject, "Long-haired Men and Short-haired Women." These subjects were in no sense themes. No process of reasoning can justify calling a topic like any of the above a sermonic theme. One can readily identify the passages of Scripture on which topics like the first two were based. It will be recognized that they are negative and not Christian. But even if they were positive and Christian, they are not themes.

Sermon subjects are often chosen for publicity value in newspaper notices or church bulletins. If the text is to be Hebrews 13:8, "Jesus Christ is the same yesterday and today, yea and forever," as per American Standard Version, the topic of the sermon could be what James Moffat entitled a book, "Jesus Christ the Same." But a preacher might choose to catch the public eye with a question, such as, "Does Christianity Need an Undertaker?" or, "Is Christianity On The Way Out?" or "Is Christ Through?" It must be kept in mind,

31

however, that in discussing the matter of a theme, the reference
is not to subject or topic, but to the clearly expressed central
truth or proposition of a sermon.

A preacher, being under the most solemn obligation to preach
the Word of God, is by so much under the abiding necessity
of finding out what the main idea of a Scripture verse or
passage is. He will read and reread verse or passage again
and again, in as many versions and languages as possible, always bent on getting an answer to his inquiry. "What does it
say and what does it mean?"

When a preacher has decided what it is a Scripture passage
teaches, he then faces the task of weighing its contemporaneous
interest and relevance. He now asks, "What is God's message
to me, to my congregation, to humanity, in this portion of
Scripture?" He is not interested only in deciding just what
it is the chosen text teaches, but how the essential truth of it
may be stated persuasively to the contemporary world.

No matter how small the congregation is, it is best for a
preacher to preach to humanity and the ages, to think not
primarily of personalities but of mankind. We mean to say
that it is a fine thing to express the theme, if possible, as a
universal. The poet Tennyson speaks of "jewels five words
long that on the stretched forefinger of time sparkle forever."
It may be that eight or ten or twelve or fifteen words are
needed, but the effort should be made to put some great truth
of Scripture into every sermon, to express it in a form easily
remembered and of general, timeless, universal appeal and
interest.

The important thing is to begin to construct the theme as
soon as the necessary study has been done to gain insight
and build up background. A first effort might consist in
writing out the heart of the message no matter how many
sentences or paragraphs it may require. Then the further
effort would consist of a process of "boiling down" what has
been written in hope of finally constructing a single sentence
of from eight to fifteen words into which the spiritual essence

of the sermon has been compressed, a sentence sufficiently polished and beautiful to grace the minds of the hearers.

The philosopher Locke likened the mind to a room and ideas to pieces of furniture. Suppose a preacher thinks of each member of his congregation as a home and of the truths he brings them in his sermons as pieces of furniture. His is the task of furnishing these homes, constituted by the personalities of his people, with the finest possible furniture. Every piece of furniture is an idea, a flash, an insight, a truth, drawn from and inspired by the Word of God. It becomes his purpose to make these homes well-furnished with every word that cometh out of the mouth of God and to make his congregation a model city of beautiful homes, a veritable city of God. It is evident that such a preacher must be a thematic preacher. Every piece of furniture his sermons provide for the minds and hearts of his people to furnish the home of the soul must be in good taste, filling a need, adding to the spiritual wealth of life, answering the prayer, "Let the beauty of the Lord our God be upon us." A preacher with such an aim will school himself in the art of true craftmanship by putting all he is and has into the construction of themes.

A professor of preaching advised his students to ask themselves a question when they had a sermon ready for the Sunday following, "What do I expect to accomplish with this sermon?" He predicted that such a practice might cause them to consign it to the waste-basket. But who wants to prepare sermons for the waste-basket? If a preacher labors and prays and sweats blood over a Bible verse or passage and over the construction of a suitable theme which, like a magnificent piece of furniture, is to have a permanent and important place in the home of the soul, he need anticipate no such frustration as to be under the necessity of filling waste-baskets with his sermons. A preacher who schools himself at all costs in theme construction and development, basing his sermons on God's revealed Word and saturating them with the redemption which is in Christ Jesus, cannot possibly be a failure either as a man or a preacher. He goes right along, leaning on the promises, a man of God and of authority, not because of human exuberance and vitality, but because God has chosen him as a channel of Divine omnipotence.

It must be repeatedly stressed that when a study of the Scripture to be expounded has yielded sufficient appropriate knowledge and background, the first thing to do is to construct the theme. The first attempt may be twenty or thirty words long. It may contain bigger words than a theme ought to have. It may be seen to be too partial in its statement of the essential truth of verse or passage. It may be minor instead of major, subordinate instead of primary.

The first effort to construct a theme for a sermon is only the beginning of resolute determination to pursue the quest of a theme by repeated reconstruction. A sentence is wanted which is worthy in content of the particular Scripture chosen and of the Bible as a whole. It must be on a level commensurate with Christianity, church history, the dignity of man, the worth of life and the needs of humanity. It must fit into a great occasion of public worship and be in keeping with the beauty of the sanctuary. It must not be a let-down after inspiring sacred music. There must be no suggestion of mental slovenliness or verbal inaptness to a congregation which has come to church spic and span in its Sunday best. If the place of worship and its appointments cannot answer to high standards of refinement and the people present share the crudeness of the environment, yet and then, if ever, must the thematic Christian preacher rise to lofty heights of spiritual vitality, and choice simple expression, laying himself out in self-effacing zeal in order that his preaching may be "in demonstration of the spirit and of power." A wise mother one day unexpectedly visited her son at college and found the walls of his room decorated with pictures of bathing beauties and actresses. She had brought with her a portrait of Christ which she put in a strategic place on the wall. When she visited the son at a later date, equally unexpectedly, the walls looked very different, but the portrait of Christ was still in evidence. When the son was asked what had happened to many of his "walled" pictures, he said, "They just did not seem to fit in with the portrait of Christ you hung on the wall." So the quality and structure of a thematic Christian sermon is never to be reduced in accommodation to human or physical environment, but if stoutly maintained, the brooding Spirit of God will bring order and beauty out of chaos and coarseness.

It is always possible to alter and improve the first theme constructed for a sermon. Write it over and over again, changing a word or a phrase, cutting out, putting in, choosing small words for big, changing the subject and predicate around, eliminating or inserting an adjective, making a new start if necessary, with more and bigger words if ingrowing thought seems to call for it. Keep on working at it. You may come, by this process, to have thirty or forty themes, constituting four or five series, each from a different angle, so that now it becomes a real question as to what idea you propose to honor as the subject in your theme. You will now be constantly reading Bible verse or passage over again and weighing the possibilities, making appraisals and decisions, presently to be reconsidered and perhaps changed. How is a preacher to get time for all this? Be of good cheer. You will be surprised how far you can get in this quest for a theme in an hour or two, if you have studied to get ready for theme construction. Moreover, you will get such joy out of it, that odd minutes, all too frequently frittered away, will now be seized, either by the forelock or the tail and be put under contribution to your noble quest.

At this and that point in your pursuit of a theme a sudden flash, some new insight, will enable you to produce a theme which will impress you at once as very much more satisfactory. At first it seems just about perfect. You try to improve it. You undertake to state it in a new way, but you may not get further than three or four words. You find that this last promising effort does not work out after all. You start over and keep right on. As indicated, an hour or two of this kind of effort often works wonders. Your idea of what you are going to preach becomes ever clearer. Your expression in theme construction moves on to greater simplicity. You may have the good fortune to attain unto a form of beauty for your Bible thought. God will certainly answer prayer as you bend yourself to constructive labor to produce a vital Christian theme in simple, and if possible, in beautiful words. You aim to produce a dynamic theme, of which your sermon will be the presentation in maturely developed form; an impressive, unforgettable theme, a theme that conveys good tidings from God, or sounds a needed alarm in a spirit and atmosphere of grace, a theme short and simple enough for old and young, a theme which enshrines a timeless, universal, Divine truth and speaks to the ages.

The right theme for a sermon is perhaps only eight words long; never, it is to be hoped, more than twelve or fifteen. The thing desired is a sentence which members of a congregation will carry home with them to ponder, to remember, to talk over with the family, to live on, to live by, to live with. It must now be said that none of the sentences framed and then found below theme standard is wasted. Apart from their service in clarifying Bible verse or passage, apart from their value in developing increasing power of original thinking, apart from their use in promoting ability to express magnificent thoughts in little words, every sentence thus written can be used in the sermon. It will fit in somewhere. It is like grist in the mill and like money in the bank.

Trial sentences in the effort to construct a strong, simple Christian theme serve very well in the introduction to the sermon. The purpose of the introduction is to state clearly the truth of Scripture to be proclaimed and unfolded. Some of the sentences written in the process of getting the right theme will function as a suitable path to the announcement of the theme. Indeed, the theme finally selected may well be, together with the rhetorical statement of the divisions, the last part of a paragraph, the other sentences of which are good, though less satisfying, ways in which the attempt was made to construct the right theme.

The idea of a theme in a Christian sermon is to give the sermon definiteness, pertinence, effectiveness, simplicity and unity. An elder once said to his minister, "Do not talk us to death." If a preacher "talks his people to death," he talks himself to death as a preacher. No congregation is going to put up with a "blitz-krieg" of mere words. It is a monstrous tragedy when a preacher is credited with having "the gift of gab."

What is the use of preaching if the people are not able to follow, if they feel moved to say that they do not know what the minister was really driving at and if they finally conclude that there is nothing to follow anyway, that the preacher in question has "nothing on the ball"? They go right on from such a reaction to blaming Christianity itself, especially if the minister is personally a "good mixer and fine fellow." They begin to consider preaching out-moded and church going "behind the times."

A preacher is not a radio news commentator. A sermon is neither an encyclopaedia article nor a rehash of current events. A sermon is a very special technique for preaching the Word of God, for preaching Christ and Him crucified, for proclaiming the Word of the Cross. A sermon that has a theme, is built on a theme and adheres to it, reiterating the theme in varied language as its unfolding proceeds, is what the very word "sermon" itself means, "a thrust." It is a thrust of the Sword of the Spirit which is the Word of God. "For the word of God is living, and active, and sharper than any two-edged sword, and piercing even to the dividing of soul and spirit, of both joints and marrow, and quick to discern the thoughts and intents of the heart."

It is true that God can and does use sermons, defective in proper structure, to do His saving work. It is not by might or power of sermon structure that souls are saved, but by the regenerating power of the Holy Spirit in the Word preached. Nevertheless, the results of much so-called preaching show the futility of preaching which ignores Biblical substance and true sermon structure. At best, many sermons are like sheet lightning which lights up things for just a moment and then leaves all in darkness again. The heart of true sermon structure is a theme, which in varied forms comes to reiterated expression, as the sermon unfolds it. The theme of a Christian sermon is like the theme or motif of a classic symphony. A thematic Christian sermon is like a bolt of lightning that hits a mark. It is a saving stab from God right through the heart, conveying resurrection life to a slain self. Thematic Christian preaching on a wide scale would storm the ramparts of evil with dynamite from God, filling the sky with the chained lightning of God's marvelous grace in Christ and striking down the enemies of God with "bolts from the blue," reducing the citadels of man's totalitarian self-will to shattered dust and replacing vaunted structures of human folly with what Paul calls "God's husbandry, God's building." When will the church of God awake to make total war on a doomed world, clergy and laity living and proclaiming one mighty testimony of the grace of God that brings salvation?

If the production of thematic Christian sermons can be compared to the manufacture of furniture and a thematic Christian sermon can be likened unto the power of an electrical storm with chained lightning illuminating the dark night of the soul and bolts of Divine grace bringing the self-life to death and resurrection in Christ, it may not be without value to compare theme and sermon construction to the making of demolition bombs and the preacher to a Superfortress, always remembering that a true sermon is a bomb of grace intended to blast souls into the Kingdom of God without violence to the exercise of moral freedom. Such symbolism has regard to the sermon and the preacher and is intended to stress importance of preacher and preaching in a streamlined civilization reverting to paganism.

When a preacher thinks of his congregation, however, he will do well to think of them also as a group of souls to be fed and of himself as God's dietitian. It is a lovely figure to think of the church of Christ as the redeemed family of God and of each congregation also as God's family. When

God entrusts a part of His redeemed family to the care of a pastor, the minister is under very definite orders to feed the flock; that is, to see to it that every member of the family gets the right kind of spiritual food and enough of it. Well may a minister constantly visualize his people, the children, the young people, the men and women in the full strength of years, the dear folks on the sunset trail. A preacher is without excuse if he preaches to adults only. No wonder boys and girls protest against going to church and if forced to do so, keep wriggling in their seats, chewing gum and looking at the clock, laying up sinister impressions, determining that when they grow up, they will give a wide berth to what was forced on them. What a fine cook and provider the thematic Christian preacher becomes when the milk and meat of God's Word becomes in his hands the necessary nourishing vitamin-laden food his church family needs, prepared with all necessary knowledge and skill to satisfy the soul's hunger and thirst for God, be it the soul of child, youth, parent or grandparent. Thematic Christian preaching is the true minister's response to Christ's prescription, "Feed my lambs! Feed my sheep!"

## IV

## Thematic Searchlights on Sermon Structure

THE theme of a Christian sermon is the initial and fundamental factor in the organization of a preacher's thought into a structure possessing unity, progress, balance, symmetry and purpose. As to unity, modern folks may be like grasshoppers in their request for a full and satisfying life, jumping from one thing to another to taste the pleasures of life, but when it comes to listening to a sermon which is just a collection of thoughts without thematic center and centripetal divisions, they are poor jumpers who stray like sheep. Vital contact between preacher and hearers may not even be established by an unthematic sermon, or if it is, it is soon broken, the mind of the hearer wanders and the sermon proves "a wholesome soporific" or wearisome.

A preacher of international fame was selected to preach the closing Sunday evening sermon of the summer season at a famous American seaside resort. Over eight thousand people crowded the huge auditorium. The preacher announced neither subject nor text nor theme. Over one hundred ushers were distributed throughout the building, each one charged with noting the number present in his section and to be on hand for eventualities. The preacher talked calmly, saying good things, but the majority of those present were unable to sense what it was he was saying. People began to whisper to one another, asking questions like this, "When is he going to start to preach?" "Why does he not tell us what he is talking about?" "Isn't this awful?" Presently the big auditorium was buzzing with the sound of many voices. Soon people began to go out. Each usher, it was learned later, kept count in his own section of those who left. The number of those who went out increased to an alarming extent. Vacant areas began to appear. At last it was over. Around all the exits, some thirty in number, people stood in groups discussing the preacher and his failure to preach. "Did you ever hear anything worse?" said one and "Why did they ever get such a man?" The ushers got their figures together and reported that over two thousand people had walked out of that auditorium during the sermon. It may be doubted whether anything like that ever happened before or since in America. What was the matter? The preacher said plenty of good things. He had a great mind and a great heart. There was a point to his sermon but it was not expressed in a specific, short, simple theme and there was no systematic exposition of the point of the sermon. When the sermon was well on its way, the preacher tied his thought to a verse of Scripture, but the congregation did not sense that the verse alluded to was the text and that the sermon was intended to be an exposition of an idea drawn from that verse. It is perhaps due partly to what happened that night that one who was present called to mind what the preacher said when it was over and tried to defend the great man by explaining the point of the sermon to his critics. This defender of the famous preacher has lived on the truth conveyed by that sermon with increasing realization of its value. But the sermon was not properly organized. It lacked a definite subject, there was no preliminary announcement of Scripture text and no introduction culminating in stating the theme of the sermon and the lines of thought along which the theme was to be unfolded. The sermon presented some ideas as a butcher might hand a string of sausages to a customer. Each sausage was good, but there was no organic unity in the sermon; the sermon was not a living organism which would bleed if you cut it. No one of the two thousand people who walked out of that auditorium would agree that the sermon contained one good sausage. Only a proper theme can bring even a sausage to deserved honor, if the sausage is an idea in a sermon that lacks organization.

It is a striking thing that structural defects in sermons can be illustrated from the sermons and preaching of the greatest preachers of our day. One such preached on "the Ascension." He stated his topic at the outset but added that he did not know just what Bible verse to choose for a text, because there were several which would be appropriate. However, he felt that the Scripture passage read in the service was as good as any. The preacher began by calling attention to the neglect of the doctrine of the Ascension in current preaching. To emphasize this he mentioned occasions when he had preached on the subject and the reactions of those who heard the sermon. This constituted his apology for preaching it again in July before a resort congregation of five thousand people. He went on to say that he did not mean to neglect other doctrines. Other doctrines were then mentioned seriatim and the preacher assured the people he did not mean to neglect them. Then he proceeded to give three points elaborating the result of the Ascension of Christ. The three points portrayed the ascended Christ as a glorified man, an interceding priest and sovereign Lord. The preacher was able, dynamic, a fine speaker, but the sermon lacked a theme. The three points were not developments of aspects of one theme.

This preacher might maintain that he did have a theme, that his theme was the Ascension of Christ, and that it was his purpose to present the practical significance of the Ascension. One is not disposed to contend with such an able preacher and such a fine Christian gentleman. A topic, however, is not a theme. It may suggest or inspire a theme. The preacher did have a purpose, but if this had been compressed into a summary statement, so that no one could miss it, the sermon would have gained immensely in unity and strength.

It occurs to the author to venture a theme offhand so that one can apply to it the principles already enunciated and finally arrive at a theme which is short, simple and dynamic. No one starts out in this matter with perfection. The first endeavor is quite sure to be too long. Here is one effort to

serve as a starter: "The Ascension of Christ is His coronation as Saviour and Lord of man." A theme of thirteen words
to start with is so far so good. The words "ascension" and
"coronation" are big words. The words "ascension" and
"coronation" used in reference to Christ are no bigger or
harder than the word inauguration applied to a man elected
president of the United States. They may have to be retained
and explained. But every preacher can do as he pleases about
it. In the interest of varied expression, other words may be
introduced into a succession of sentences calculated to make
real what actually happened when Christ ascended and how
significant it was. It is possible that you might write a sentence like this: "The risen Christ went up to heaven to carry
on as Saviour and Lord." These fourteen words are all
simple. In between the first suggested theme and this last
one, you might use different words for coronation in as many
sentences, like, "investment with power," "certification,"
"authentification," "crowning," "assumption of authority." If
the bigger of these words do nothing else, they serve as fresh
starters for renewed efforts to be simple and to hit upon all
sorts of ways to make the truth clear and to make it tell.

Continuing to concentrate on this matter of the ascension
of Christ, you may possibly feel moved to ask questions. After
all, what you are after is a message for today. It occurs to
you that a pertinent question for the contemporary world is,
"Where Is Christ Now?" For church notice in newspaper or
announcement in church bulletin, you may prefer this question
as the subject of the sermon. It has more publicity appeal
in it than the topic, "The Ascension." You decide on "Where
Is Christ Now?" as your subject. It seems best to fashion the
theme in harmony with the topic and you write one, "Christ
is now in heaven as Saviour and Lord of men." Persisting
in concentrated meditation, you begin to question whether the
word "now" is needed. The shorter a theme, the better.
That holds for a topic also. Care must be exercised not to
reduce the meaning and power of either topic or theme. You
venture on revision. You select as topic, "Where Is Christ?"

and as theme, "Christ is in heaven as Lord and Saviour."
Unconsciously you left off the words "of man." It goes without saying that Christ's Lordship and Saviourhood refer to
humanity. You find to your joy that the theme has only eight
words.

Suppose, then, that we propose to preach on the Ascension
of Christ. We crave a topic which will give us a chance to
describe the nature of the ascension and its meaning for today
and the ages. A topic is needed which will excite public
interest. We crave also a theme which will compress the
meaning of the Ascension of Christ for today into a short,
simple, unforgettable, dynamic sentence. The topic, "Where
Is Christ?" is short, Christian, constructive, appealing, simple.
A child can understand it. Every Christian ought to be interested in it. One not a Christian may be moved to wonder
what the answer to such a question will be. "Christ is in
heaven as Lord and Saviour" is also clear, short, definite, relevant, constructive, Christian and ought to be good as theme.

Now, as to the divisions, that is to say, the development
of the theme in the body of the sermon. It has been suggested
that the divisions be stated both rhetorically and logically,
that is, to announce the division first as topic and then in a
sentence. We now add that the divisions may be indicated
by questions. The question would be stated in each case before
the rhetorical and logical statements. The reference now is
to each division as the preacher gets to it. If a preacher
chooses to announce his divisions all together at the close of
the introduction of the sermon, just after he has announced
his theme, he need give only either the questions or the rhetorical statements of the divisions. The logical statement of
the divisions should be given only at the beginning of the
division following the rhetorical statement of it. If questions
are announced by the preacher after the statement of the theme
and before stating the divisions rhetorically, the appropriate
question should also introduce each division, followed by the
rhetorical and logical statement of that division.

Take, now, the theme, "Christ is in heaven as Lord and Saviour." We propose to venture on the introduction of a sermon on the Ascension of Christ with the theme as stated. This is how the sermon might start:

The subject of the sermon is, "Where Is Christ?" based on the book of "The Acts," chapter one, verses nine to eleven. These verses we now read in your hearing. (The text is read.) This is the story of the ascension of Jesus and contains a promise of His return. Our present interest is in the ascension of Jesus as furnishing the answer to the question, "Where Is Christ?"

Jesus is the most important person who has ever lived on this earth. What he said and did and was will always have meaning. Jesus is never out of date. His value to humanity is for the ages. It is therefore always a timely and living question, "Where Is Christ?" What happened to Jesus after He was crucified, dead and buried? Was that the end of Jesus, of One whose surpassing significance is written so deeply into the life of mankind? The resurrection of Jesus and His ascension into heaven answer the question, "What happened to Jesus?" The ascension of Jesus into heaven more definitely answers the question, "Where is Christ?" Christ is in heaven as our Divine Redeemer. The truth sings itself into the soul as a theme-song, "Christ is in heaven as Lord and Saviour."

It is well to go into the matter. Christ is in heaven as Lord and Saviour. It is fitting to ask, "How did Christ get to Heaven?" and "Why did Christ go to heaven?" The question proposed was, "Where Is Christ?" The New Testament story of the ascension of Jesus supplies the answer, "Christ is in heaven as Lord and Saviour." Two further questions bring us to the heart of the answer, "How did Christ get to heaven?" and "Why did Christ go to heaven?" To answer these questions and experience the power of the theme requires consideration, first, of the nature and reality of the ascension; and secondly, of the purpose of the ascension.

First, then, How did Christ get to heaven? or the nature

and the reality of the ascension of Jesus. Christ got into heaven by ascension. The risen Lord ascended into heaven. It was a real historical event that had time, place and occasion. Let us go over the record picturing to ourselves just how it was, what really happened and how wonderful it was. Etc., etc.

Now, secondly, Why did Christ ascend into heaven? Consider the purpose of the Ascension. Jesus ascended into heaven in order to take His great power and reign as the Divine Redeemer. The Ascension is Christ's coronation as Lord and Saviour. Christ went up into heaven forty days after His resurrection to serve as King and Redeemer and rule with sovereign grace. The truth here has several aspects which may be successively unfolded for instruction, comfort and inspiration. Etc., etc.

At this point, subdivisions of the second division may be listed as follows and then elaborated in due succession;

(a.) Christ went to heaven to assume active sovereignty as the rightful King of humanity.

(b.) Christ went to heaven to function as the Divine Redeemer of the world.

(c.) Christ went to heaven to fulfill a priestly ministry of unceasing intercession.

(d.) Christ went to heaven to make Pentecost possible.

(e.) Christ went to heaven to prepare the promised eternal home for His redeemed people.

Please observe that in the sample introduction given for a sermon on the Ascension of Christ, the outline of the sermon was given to the extent of stating the two main divisions first in the form of questions and then rhetorically. A paragraph was also given to indicate how each division might be undertaken. Note that at the beginning of each division the question to be developed was given, followed by the rhetorical statement of what the division is to develop and this in turn followed by a logical statement or "sentence form" of the development to be expected in the division.

If a preacher qualifies himself by study as already indicated, subdivisions like those suggested will find him possessed of the necessary resources to portray the heavenly life of our adorable and sovereign Saviour with cumulative power. No telling what further original ideas he may be able to introduce to serve as God's dietitian to his congregation.

What about the conclusion? Every sermon must have a conclusion which brings the thought to a climax. How would something like the following do?

"O the wonder of it and the grace of it that one like Jesus is in the place of power! The world today knows what happens when bad men get great power. No one can measure what has been suffered by innocent people from brutal dictators. Who ever would have conceived it possible that human beings could inflict such savage horrors on fellow human beings? One can but be lost in wonder, love and praise when it is given him to see that Jesus reigns, that ultimate destinies are in Christ's hands, that the universe is built on the principle of self-giving love. Unspeakable is the comfort of realizing the Lordship of our Divine Redeemer.

"The future of every man is in Christ. 'Now is the accepted time, now is the day of salvation.' 'Softly and tenderly Jesus is calling.' 'Today if you hear his voice, harden not your heart.' 'Come, sinner, come.' Let every Christian from this moment on give Christ His crown in personal life and labor to get Christ His crown at the hands of all men. 'Jesus shall reign.' All who are in Him shall reign with Him. 'Halleluiah, what a Saviour!' "

Every thematic Christian preacher out of his own raptured heart will know how to conclude a sermon that has been the unfolding of a lofty Scriptural theme. When a sermon is a unity and becomes the carrying out of specific aim and purpose, the preacher "kicks a goal," has the time of his life preaching, radiates a joyous contagious Christian atmosphere and is used of God to do his people good and lead souls to Christ. It may serve now to exhibit the outline presented for the reader's examination and appraisal.

*Sermon Subject*: Where is Christ?

*Scripture Basis*: Acts 1 :9-11

*Theme*: Christ is in heaven as Lord and Saviour.

*Divisions*:

I. How did Christ get to heaven? (Stated as a question)
The Nature and Reality of the Ascension. (Stated rhetorically)
Christ got into heaven by Ascension. (Stated logically)

II. Why did Christ ascend into heaven? (Stated as a question)
The Purpose of the Ascension. (Stated rhetorically)
Jesus ascended into heaven in order to take His great power and reign as the Divine Redeemer. (Stated logically)

*Subdivisions* (Stated logically only):

(a.) Christ went to heaven to rule as King.

(b.) Christ went to heaven to serve as Divine Redeemer.

(c.) Christ went to heaven to offer priestly intercession.

(d.) Christ went to heaven to make Pentecost possible.

(e.) Christ went to heaven to get it ready for His redeemed people.

*Conclusions*:

All things are in Christ's power. What a Saviour!

A preacher might prefer to use the name "Jesus" in the above outline. That would be very much to the point. The Bible verses on which the sermon is based use the name Jesus. "This Jesus, who was received up from you into heaven," says the text. When we use the name Christ it is natural to mean "Christ the Lord." When we use the name Jesus, it is natural to add the word Saviour and say, "Jesus, Saviour." In the context the disciples address the risen Jesus as Lord. The narrative presents Jesus Christ the Lord and Saviour of mankind as departing in the body of His glory and being received into heaven. It may be the intention of the record to impress that the resurrection and ascension of Jesus mark the permanent incorporation of Jesus' humanity into His Deity. His glorified resurrection form is "the first-fruits of them that sleep" and is thus prophetic of the ultimate coronation of redeemed humans.

Why go on talking about the Ascension of Jesus when an outline of a thematic sermon on it has already been presented? The answer is that we are also demonstrating a technique for the pursuit of a theme and for the construction of thematic sermon outlines. The outline presented is not as satisfactory as it might be. The reason is that the development of the sermon body goes beyond the passage which serves as text. There is no law against doing that. The use of parallel passages is always in order. The proposed sermon is topical. A topical sermon is one that draws its topic from the text but not the divisions. There is no reason why a topical sermon should not be thoroughly Biblical and the development outlined on the Ascension is Biblical and thematic. The sermon proposed is not only topical but doctrinal, being constructed to convey the reality and nature and the significance of the ascension of Jesus. Adhering to Bible teaching as it does and drawing on parallel and other pertinent Scriptures, especially in the subdivisions of the second division, the sermon would also be expository. This makes it necessary to say that while text-books on sermon construction distinguish sermons as topical, textual, narrative, expository, doctrinal and evangelistic, in actual pastoral thematic preaching, these distinctions are not mutually exclusive. A more fundamental discrimination insists on sermons being Scriptural and thematic. This guarantees milk and meat from God's Word in a form suited to all ages and appetites.

# V

## Structural Aspects of Thematic Sermons

A DEFINITE theme, a real Christian theme, clearly and succinctly expressed, guarantees unity in a sermon because the preacher is pursuing a specific goal as he unfolds it. One of the latest wonders of science is a motor one and one half inches square which is able to lift an airplane elevator. So a good sermon theme is able to lift a sermon into the atmosphere of clear vision of its aim. "The lamp of the body is the eye"; the lamp of a sermon is the theme. "If therefore thine eye be single, thy whole body shall be full of light." Similarly, if thy theme be single, thy whole sermon shall be full of light.

The theme is a truth, drawn from the Word of God, which has gripped the soul of the preacher. Only a thematic Christian preacher can tell what travail of soul it represents, through what dark ways of toil and sweat, he has at last reached a mountain-top of vision and what joy of discovery has been granted him in the prayerful, industrious study of God's self-revelation in Christ.

The preacher knows that what the thematic truth has done for him it can do for others. He is conscious of being an instrument as well as beneficiary of "the Guiding Light" and a channel of regenerating power from God. He labors and prays to see that power operative in the lives of those to whom he ministers. His attitude is expressed by the words of the apostle James, "Receive with meekness the implanted word, which is able to save your souls." It is his to set forth the testimony of God's self-revelation. He does it with holy passion in the assured hope that God's Word will not return unto Him void, but shall accomplish that which God pleases and prosper in the thing whereto God sent it (Isa. 55:10, 11).

The development of the thought of a sermon must be marked by progress. A good sermon theme is of immeasurable service in promoting progressing thought. The theme is like the shot that means, "Go." The theme expresses the purpose and sets the goal. A good sermon theme provides the directing idea, maps out the course to be pursued, the point to be reached, the heights to be scaled, the climax to be achieved. A preacher is not going to linger and loiter when he knows where he is going and where he would take his congregation. He will not be tempted to multiply mere words so as to occupy the allotted time. He will not spin out his sermon to inordinate length under the false notion that he has to keep on talking because he is not saying anything. Many a preacher must admit to himself that his longest sermons have been those when he had least to say. Straight as an arrow to its target is the progress of a sermon to its goal if the sermon is properly constructed to bring home to the hearts of the hearers a theme which is God's speech to the lost and elect.

A sermon theme deftly and definitely explored as per Scripture revelation in a given verse or passage insures balance and symmetry in sermon construction. The divisions of a thematic sermon are all aspects of the theme, promoting observance of the law of proportion, occupying the same relation to the body of a sermon that wheels do to a chassis. Cars without wheels are found in junk yards and are no longer cars whatever semblance of body may remain. So a sermon requires a theme and a theme calls for appropriate division so that the body of the sermon gets something to move on and can be sent with speed, dispatch and impact to a shining goal.

Balance and symmetry are much more readily obtainable in a sermon constructed thematically than in a sermon which represents a collection of thoughts. How easy it is for a themeless preacher to devote two-thirds of his preaching time in a Sunday service to one third of the subject. One preacher who made constant use of homiletic aids has been known to jot down thoughts or illustrations and to put after each a figure indicating how long in terms of minutes he thought he could make that particular story or idea in his Sunday sermon. Thus a thought or illustration might be marked "two minutes," "three minutes," "five minutes." That is preaching by the clock with a vengeance. Such a preacher may even preach with a purpose, the purpose to get it over with.

Here, then, are the marks of a properly constructed sermon, each deserving the name of "principle," the principle of unity, of progress, of balance and symmetry, of purpose and chosen goal, principles which hold a preacher to a theme and to its development according to the principles set forth. A thematic Christian preacher discovers that the occurrence of a thought to his mind is no inevitable ticket of admission to a sermon. A preacher has a task to fulfill, a way to pursue, a goal to reach, a target to hit, a responsibility to discharge, a war to wage, glad tidings to herald, the Christ to preach, a revelation of God to proclaim and expound, lost souls to save, weak saints to edify, strong saints to inspire, a testimony to give, reality to portray, a Saviour to commend, rash sinners to warn, and sufferers and bereaved to heal and comfort. Thematic Christian preaching is the therapeutic implementation of God's healing grace. It is the right kind of preaching for a vagrant age and race implementing Christ's seeking to save. Thematic Christian preaching hits the nail on the head. It is man to man preaching that reaches all sorts and conditions of men because God's self-revelation in Christ covers all ages, races, conditions, problems and needs, being designed to meet our total human predicament.

Thematic Christian preaching, resting as it does for substance on the Word of God and for technique on the sermonic form of proclamation comes perhaps under the category of what the world contemptuously calls the foolishness of God and the weakness of God, but the thematic Christian preacher knows that "the foolishness of God is wiser than men" and "the weakness of God is stronger than men." In this realm of thematic Christian preaching, God uses things that are not to bring to nought things that are. Therefore he is of good hope. He knows that over wide areas of human life, the inner light has failed, and that the light which is in men has become darkness. The pressure on the modern mind, multiplicity of interests, activities and pleasures, vitiation of moral atmosphere by trampling Divine imperatives and sanctions in the mire, the rebelliousness of the human spirit toward righteousness and goodwill, the present-day fall of man and reversion to paganism, all these call for clear voices in a wilderness of frustration and disintegration. The thematic Christian preacher regards himself with warrant as God's instrument for blasting the citadels of man's antagonism to God, bringing bread from God to famished souls in areas occupied by God's enemies.

No man renders a greater service to humanity than a thematic Christian preacher. He sweats blood over sermon construction as he does in the labor of mastering God's Word and shepherding Christ's flock. He studies and grinds as if it is all up to him. He prays and weeps before the Lord as if he cannot do a thing. He is a Trojan for work and he casts himself like a broken and empty vessel at God's feet, praying for Pentecostal power to be worthy of his vocation.

There are sermons in stones and brooks, but there should be themes in all sermons and a message from God's Word in both sermon and theme. Better forget the stones and brooks unless you know your Bible well enough to have a stone tell you about the Church's one foundation and a brook remind you of the river of God's pleasures and of the Fountain of life that shoots its living waters high for all dead souls who put their trust in Christ.

The idea of a theme is to avoid irrelevance in preaching. A preacher can literally roam all over the world, all over history, all over the universe, all over the Bible, all over the sciences and the arts and literature and current events, if he does not have a theme and a thematically developed sermon. It is conceivable that a sermon might have a theme and not be thematically developed. One asked another about a certain preacher, "Did he have a text?" The answer was, "Yes, but if the text had had smallpox, the sermon would not have caught it." We plead for a sermon theme, for a thematic sermon thematically developed and for thematic Christian preaching. One who does the necessary studying, thinking and praying to produce a theme in the manner herein described will by so much have that much inducement and headway and resource to be true to the theme and develop it. You have to stick to the Bible for Christian themes and to your Christian themes to preach the Bible thematically.

Thematic Christian preaching is to be preaching of the Bible in its total, drastic, revolutionary, redemptive, comprehensive significance. If a preacher presents a sermon on the words, "And David danced before the ark," he almost forfeits the right to be called a Christian preacher. In the interest of a spurious originality and a futile variety, a preacher has been known to take the word "But" as the text 'for a sermon, from the words, "But Naaman was a leper." Such a procedure, however well-meaning, appears on the surface disgraceful. There has been a lot of mighty poor preaching and a preacher puts himself in a welcome light if he majors on rich, juicy Bible verses, paragraphs and chapters, for his nourishing, vitamin-laden, substantial, heaven-born, thematic Christian sermons.

Even a clown must know that not every word or clause or sentence in the Bible is intended for sermonic use. There is a main trend in the Bible. Its infallibility is what A. B. Davidson called "the infallibility of common sense." There are great pure streams of Divine revelation. George Adam Smith wrote a critical commentary on Isaiah and other Old Testament prophets. But how that great critical scholar could revel in the magnificent and majestic spiritual conceptions he encountered! His soul got so on fire that he would insert into his exposition a rapturous thanksgiving or doxology.

Let every preacher study what it is to use the Word of God deceitfully. Let any preacher who thus makes the Word of God ridiculous know that he must bear his share of responsibility for the disrepute of the American pulpit, for the drift away from the Church and for current contempt of Christianity.

All Christian preaching must serve the end of deliverance out of our human predicament, further man's acceptance of God's offered grace in Christ, register as a factor, a campaign, a battle, a sally, in the Divine crusade of redemption. To this end, major on preaching the immensities of God's redeeming love. Live in the heights. Walk humbly with God. Keep the soul-fires burning by living close to the heart of God. Lean constantly on Jesus' breast. Give Him the freedom of the house of life. "Sanctify in your hearts Christ Jesus as Lord." Shame on us, Christian preachers, unless in preaching we specialize on big, significant, revealing, creative verses and passages of Scripture and with sweat and tears and blood distil their essence into themes and thematic Christian sermons. Out of such Christian themes and thematic Christian sermons will radiate the fragrance of God's offered grace in Christ. "The story must be told" and when it is told, proclaimed, expounded and persuasively presented by men whose lives are transcripts of it, whose hearts are on fire to win a lost world for Christ, who yearn to stimulate Christians as they climb the steep ascent of heaven, it does the work God has entrusted to preachers and preaching, even if the preachers have to become fools for Christ's sake and the world calls the preaching foolishness.

The thematic Christian preacher is sustained by the assurance that it still pleases God by the foolishness of preaching to save such as believe. It is his part to specialize on "the testimony of Christ," to preach Christ in all the value of His self-revelation, concentrating shafts of heavenly light into summary heart-warming themes, to be exploded in sermons evincing the power of God's grace. All the parts of a thematic Christian sermon are precision parts, constructed in the liberty which proves the presence of the Holy Spirit but nevertheless framed with inspired nicety to open blind eyes, pierce deaf ears, purge bad hearts, melt hard ones and create life under the ribs of death.

# VI

## Surplus Values of Theme Construction

THE effort to state the gist of a sermon in a sentence and to construct the entire sermon in elaboration of the message thus briefly epitomized is subject to the law of unearned increment and yields by-products of the highest value. The construction of a sermon theme after due scholarly preparation is always the result of a developed ability in the sphere of the Bible verse or passage selected.

The study of the Scripture chosen for a sermon is always a quest of exploration in hope of discovery and at the same time a voyage of prayer in the spirit of the Psalmist, "Send out thy light and thy truth, let them lead me; And let them bring me to thy holy hill." It is a venture in both intellectual and spiritual search. If one will not do the work required and draw industriously on the stores of Christian knowledge available, there is little use in praying for that which requires a combination of work and prayer. If one works and works but does not pray, many an intellectual treasure may be gathered without experiencing its real riches. Facts can be awfully cold and distant, like a seventeen-year locust when it has had only ten years of sleep. The results of Christian scholarship only live or become alive in Christian preachers when the price paid includes believing dependence on God. The right kind of quest for a Christian sermon theme is bound to make the Christian preacher a scholarly man and a man of spiritual understanding and power.

When a preacher is busy covering his sources, extracting if possible their wealth of meaning, experiencing difficulty perhaps in laying hold of what is vital, he keeps asking and imploring, "Just what have we here? What do these words say? What do they mean? What do they have to do with life today?" Such persistent inquiry makes for open mental eyes, develops power to think, to study, to estimate, to decide. What better way is there for a preacher or layman to learn to know the mind of God, to gain factual knowledge of the Bible and to visualize it as an operative illuminating, regenerating, cleansing and sustaining power in terms of radiant, victorious and dynamic Christian living? When a preacher gets to see that there is more to a well-known passage than he ever saw in it before, there comes to be more and more to such a preacher, too, than anybody had yet realized. When a preacher gets first-hand knowledge of the greatness of the Word of God, his personal life is expanded, deepened and strengthened by the experience. God's greatness comes into such a man's little-ness and both preacher and congregation have a "great" time. Power to study, to think, to see, to understand, to say, to do, to become, is implicit in the process by which the Christian preacher pursues the toilful climb to heights of spiritual vision. Mounts of vision are always areas of spacious clarity and far horizons, rich in by-products, surplus and unearned increments.

Preparation for thematic Christian preaching takes care of all intellectual interests of the preacher, such as the development of scholarly habits, the acquisition of appropriate Christian knowledge, growing acquaintance with other pertinent fields of knowledge, sharpening of all mental faculties, general alertness and sensitiveness to everything that may serve God in sermons, originality in conception and expression, simplicity and beauty in style of utterance and assured progress in general scholarly competence. The higher the price you pay for a theme, the bigger the bonus.

No doubt greater facility in theme construction comes with practice but do not presume. A seminary graduate was ordained and installed as pastor of a church where three sermons were required every Sunday. He was instructed in the art and science of thematic Christian preaching. He started out to preach as he was taught. He was unable to see it through with three new sermons to prepare every week. When he was on the verge of a nervous break-down, he gave up the attempt to get a theme for every sermon and then to develop the sermon thematically. He was so wrought up and overwrought that he was brought low, as the Psalmist says. Every time he went into his pulpit, he felt unprepared. He just did not seem to have what it takes to get three thematic sermons ready every week. There ought to be a law against any preacher preaching three sermons on Sunday. It is not in any one preacher to take care of pastoral work, administrative duties, religious education in the church and in addition prepare three sermons a week and spend the necessary energy on Sunday to preach them. It may be questioned whether the same listener can really take in three sermons on a Sunday. Experienced pastors will testify that many members do not listen nearly as well at an evening service as they do in the morning.

The young minister referred to made a mistake in giving up entirely the work of thematic sermon construction. He might have stuck to it for the morning sermon only and have done the best he could for the other services. His case is referred to in order to stress what big business it is really to preach. The price has to be paid but the dividends are immense. We maintain that a minister does not really preach unless he preaches a sermon. We maintain, further, that a sermon is a very specialized form of oral presentation, a very specific, carefully defined, technique for proclaiming the Christian Gospel, which means heralding the glad tidings of God's salvation, the announcement of what God has done about the plight of man.

Ideally, a preacher ranks with an opera or motion picture star, with a concert maestro, with famous artists and sculptors. No more important work is done on earth than preaching the Christian Gospel. The required form is the sermonic and a real sermon calls for a theme, a central truth, a fundamental proposition, and is the unified, progressive, balanced, symmetrical, systematic presentation thereof in its essential, redemptive, timeless, universal import. We say that ideally a preacher ranks with the great ones of the earth. The only difference is that the preacher's work surpasses all other work in importance. Therefore it costs more to do it as it should be done. No greater need confronts the world than a revival of apostolic, Pentecostal preaching. The best brained young men have gone through our universities and into the construction of a streamlined civilization. They have passed up the Christian ministry, blind to its supreme magnificence, to the great life into which it leads, to the vast influence it promises, to the deathless fame in God's firmament of stars which faithfulness in the Christian ministry achieves. They have been unaware that the appalling plight of man is due to the secularization of life and its alliance with vulgar egoism.

Any young man who craves action, interest, scope, who wants to go places and see and do things, who wants to be on the ground floor with world builders, who is rearing to go into something big, significant, climacteric, is well-advised to become a thematic Christian preacher. He will be given a book full of dynamite, which blasts to bless, destroys to construct, and slays to resurrect. He will enter upon a life linked to omnipotence, tuned to the music of the spheres, shining with the reflected light of the Sun of righteousness and drinking of the river of God's pleasures. What a work for brilliant young men is the Christian ministry! What a field for battle and conquest is the Christian pulpit! What an instrument for reconstruction through redemption is the Christian church! Whan an implement for human salvation is a thematic Christian sermon! What sacrifices it all takes, but what benefits it confers! What labor it exacts, what sweat and blood it costs, but what rewards ensue and what surpluses enrich! The biggest man is too small for it unless he resigns from all self-importance. The smallest can make a go of it, if God gives him the Go-sign. Here all is supernatural in and through the natural. You work and slave to know it all and to construct the all of knowledge into a theme, a shaft of light, an arrow of life, a bomb of grace. "O for a theme" is the slogan and when you get it, when it flashes in on you, you know where it came

from and you sing "O for a tongue to praise my God." Thus
life alternates while the thematic Christian preacher keeps
toiling. "O for a theme!" "O for a tongue!"

Thematic Christian preaching exacts a toil which would
guarantee a revival of the lost art of meditation. When one
takes a look at the teeming life of cities or views the passing
procession of automobiles on a great highway or gazes at
the world of industry from some intersecting travel lane, it
becomes apparent that a streamlined civilization is on the
march and hitting it up on all cylinders. It bids fair to qualify
as a race of grasshoppers. No one would credit a grasshopper
with possessing an intellectual incubator. But every clergyman
must major on mental incubation. No better groundwork
can be laid for intellectual incubation than the work needed
to arrive at a dynamic sermon theme. The thematic Christian
preacher will have this experience on occasion, perhaps rather
frequently. He is hard put to it during some particular week to
cover the necessary ground in commentaries to qualify him to
write the coveted theme and sermon outline. He devotes all
the time to it at his disposal, but funerals, weddings, sick-
calls, conferences and imperative correspondence tear him away
again and again. Naturally, while he is at his books, he does
his best to concentrate with intense application. While on the
way to meet this or that appointment, he does not forget the
rapid approach of Sunday or what it was he was studying.
While he is on the go, he meditates. More and more he is
delivered from a vagrant mind or from idle fancies and things
which should have no place in a mind when a preacher has the
mind of Christ. But during this particularly extra busy week,
he assembles scattered but pertinent thoughts and ponders
notes written on his reading, but repeated efforts to write a
satisfactory theme prove unsuccessful. He does the best he
can to produce some kind of outline, but his best at present
resembles an idea or two and some illustrative thoughts or
suggestions. Not only is he unable to get down on paper what
he wants and needs, but the necessary inner light is not there.

What can a harried and hounded pastor do when Sunday comes on like a deluge and the sermon he wants is encased in glacial ice? For a preacher in such a state in such a week with such a background of honest though futile effort, it is more important to pray than to continue studying. Lay it before the Lord how busy you have been, the excessive demands on your time and strength, the honest efforts you have made to get ready for the pulpit. Implore God's help. You may be so wrought up that presently you are weeping before the Lord. You are prostrate before Him. Sunday is all but here and you are yet in no sense "there." But God answers. He speaks to you as he did to Ezekiel, "Son of man, stand upon thy feet, and I will speak to thee." God's first speech on that never-to-be forgotten Saturday night was assurance of His presence and peace and power. You received grace to leave it to God. You went to bed and slept like "a top." You awoke rather earlier than usual. A theme! A theme! It was there. The outline followed immediately. The glacier was melting in a sea of thought. You could hardly contain yourself. You did not mean to, but you woke your wife with all your goings-on. "Anything wrong, dear?" she queried. "Darling, I have my sermon." The thoughts you had gathered during the week past, the ideas cold with hidden possibilities, the illustrative suggestions, all were on fire. The morning light had broken for your soul, the darkness had disappeared, it was like "clear-shining after rain" or radiant morn and golden light ending the dark night. How God used you on that memorable Sabbath day! After a good long rest on Sunday afternoon, another similar experience made you ready for the evening service. No, it is "not by might nor by power, but by God's Spirit." But no preacher need expect such a Sunday after a lazy week. Every preacher must fill up the last full measure of devotion to his high calling, not sparing himself, working without stint, praying for grace to keep himself unspotted from the world, practicing the presence of God, keeping himself in the love of God, cultivating the fellowship with Christ into which God has called him. Paderewski, world-

famous pianist, is reported to have said that if he omitted practice for one day, he could notice a difference in his playing;
if he omitted practice for a week, his audiences noticed the
difference. Men who are charged with a prophet's call and
partake of the amazing honor of being ambassadors of Jesus
Christ must literally be "faithful unto death" in studying the
Bible, in perfecting their use of sermonic technique for Gospel
preaching and baptizing their work in constant prayer for the
grace of God in the realized presence and power of Christ.
Preachers who toe the mark will discover more and more
reasons to slough off any remaining cerements of death in
their resurrection life. That is to say, they may come to see
that certain permitted habits eloquently justified yet hinder
the giving of the utmost for the highest, and weaken Christian
testimony. Such a preacher may come to feel that even "smoke
gets in your eyes." O no, he does not intend to become a
carping critic of everybody and everything. He longs to be
what the prophet Micah was to his day and nation, when he
said, "But as for me, I am full of power by the Spirit of Jehovah, and of judgment, and of might, to declare unto Jacob
his transgression, and to Israel his sin." He longs to proclaim
the glad tidings of salvation through Jesus Christ "in demonstration of the spirit and of power." He finds that God never
lets him down. In his study of the Word and in his life of
prayer he comes to visions and revelations of the Lord. Reserve
assets increase, blessed surpluses, dynamic unearned increments, so that his pulpit experiences, his thematic Christian
sermons, become occasions of Pentecostal fervor. Why then
not operate on all cylinders with clean points and holy oil? All
a preacher has to do is to make the necessary investments, to
put all he has into it and God will see to the dividends, the
weekly, daily and life-long returns on a man's whole-souled
committal of himself to the service of Jesus Christ in the ministry of the Christian Gospel.

Thematic Christian preaching, well-done when it is the
product and expression of the necessary labor, coupled with
the blessing of God, causes a minister to be respected and

honored. That surplus value of being a workman who does not need to be ashamed redounds to the well-being of a minister's family, the peace and harmony of the church served and to the status of Christianity in the community. The satisfied customer idea has its parallel in a congregation served by a thematic Christian preacher who puts all he is and has into sermon preparation and construction.

There are Christian Communions which have organizational provision for the periodic shifting of ministers. Others find it necessary to appoint committees on pulpit exchange. Restlessness among ministers is a well-known phenomenon in modern society. Churches get sick of their ministers and ministers get sick of their churches. Studious, conscientious, prayerful preparation and delivery of thematic Christian sermons would meet this situation to a remarkable degree. Christian congregations are intended to revel in the raptures of redemption. This requires a realized salvation, a living fellowship with Christ, a being led by competent pastoral preaching into green fields and beside still waters of spiritual nurture and refreshment. A preacher will not need to look over the fence into the pastures of others if he has sense and grace enough to keep heading for perfection as an informed, alert, dynamic, thematic sermonizer. People go to church to worship God and to be fed with bread from heaven in the sanctuary. If a pastor proves himself to be the man of the hour, if he keeps faith with them, if he shows himself an expert dietitian, ministering the needed fare graded to the variety of capacity represented by a congregation, they will respect him, thank God and take courage, parents impressing upon children that Jesus satisfies. At first they may praise him and say "he has the goods," "knows his stuff," "has something on the ball." This will indicate that the preacher is on the way but has not yet arrived. When under God his sermons get them to say, "Halleluiah, what a Saviour," then he knows that they are safely bound to the triumphal chariot of Christ and finds it in himself to add a few "Halleluiahs" of his own.

The greater simplicity of utterance which rewards a minister's study of the Word and his thematic quest yields a clearer understanding of the Christian Gospel, a more concrete and more easily understood and felt presentation of it in thematic sermonic form, a more intelligent response and so a constant elevation of preacher and congregation into higher reaches of Christian realization and expression. They may forget everything of a hymn except the first line because they have so much reason to sing it, "Somebody came and lifted me." How wonderful occasions of public worship are when the thematic Christian preacher can make it so plain and compelling that people feel the undergirding of the everlasting arms of God's mercy. Such a preacher has the answer to his prayer, "Make me a channel of blessing."

# VII

## The Birth of a Thematic Sermon

THE preacher who fulfils the requirements for adequate sermon preparation is at any moment apt to come to "visions and revelations of the Lord" and to be in on the birth of a sermon. You never can tell at what moment a word or phrase or sentence will leap up, as it were, out of the study of the Scriptures and stand in your presence as an angel of light.

Here, for example, is a verse that records one of the resurrection appearances of our Lord, recorded in Mark 16:12, "And after these things he was manifested in another form unto two of them as they walked, on their way into the country." It occurs to you to associate this with a longer account in Luke 24:13-35. But the words which now somehow stand out are the words "another form." Presently you are thinking of the word "form." Suddenly the great Christological passage in Paul's Epistle to the Philippians comes to mind. The law of association does you a good turn by bringing in this other Scripture where the word "form" is twice found. You are reading Philippians 2:5-11. "Have this mind in you, which was also in Christ Jesus, who, existing in the form of God, counted not the being on an equality with God a thing to be grasped, but emptied himself, taking the form of a servant, being made in the likeness of men; and being found in fashion as a man, he humbled himself, becoming obedient even unto death, yea, the death of the cross." etc.

You are beginning to feel that you are in touch with something immense. "This Jesus" before "the days of His flesh" had his being in "the form of God." When He came to earth He took upon himself "the form of a servant." After His

65

crucifixion, He appeared in "another form." You recall a book with the title *Jehovah-Jesus* in which the author searches the Scriptures in order to show that the Jehovah of the Old Testament is the Jesus of the New Testament. You set what you have in order before the eyes of your mind and heart. "The form of God," preincarnate self-revelation in the Jehovah of the Old Testament, the incarnate Christ in the form of a bond-servant and the risen Christ in "another form."

It dawns upon you, of course, that "this Jesus" is an eternal being, that at all times he has everything well in hand and that it is He Himself Who determines fact and form of self-manifestation. Reverently you imagine yourself in His preincarnate presence. He is telling you way back there in eternity of a prodigal world and His purpose to redeem rebel mankind. He lets you in on just how He means to go about it. You learn that there is a light that lighteth every man because he who exists in "the form of God" has manifested Himself in the spiritual structure and conscience of human personality. He informs you of His purpose to become incarnate, to enter into the lot of man as Redeemer by the gateway of birth. It is laid before you how he proposes to lay down that incarnate life for the salvation of men and to make it the one perfect sacrifice for sins forever. You ask, "Will your death remove you from the earth forever?" Christ says it will not. He promises to show Himself alive in another form, in different forms to different people. He promises further to take up His abode with His followers, to make the hearts of believers His home by the power of the Holy Spirit. He adds that He will one day return visibly in glorious majesty to wind things up as far as mortal existence is concerned.

You never thought of Christianity just in this way before. You are coming to see that all the acts of Christ are acts of an eternal Being, that He is able to manifest Himself in more than one form, in forms suitable to the human situation, that the different forms of His self-manifestation are predetermined to the carrying out of His redemptive work and to the needs of those who have put their trust in Him. This leads you to conclude that institutions, movements, churches and individuals may serve as forms of Christ's self-manifestation.

Paul's teaching about the Church as the body of Christ now stands in a fresh light. All Christians are ideally the present form of Christ's self-manifestation. Every Christian is a member of the body of Christ, necessary to Christ, living for Him and through Him. But you know your church history, you know that the Church has its ups and downs, that there have been periods of sin and shame, of diminishing and all but spent witness, when Christ has appeared in "another form" to make a new start as it were. God raised up a Martin Luther, a John Calvin, a John Wesley, a Dwight L. Moody, a William Booth to be another form of the eternal Christ's self-manifestation. You are thinking also of such movements as the Sunday School, the Salvation Army, the modern Missionary Enterprise, the Christian Endeavor, the Student Volunteers, and the Youth for Christ, movements representative of new forms of Christ's self-manifestation. You are saying to yourself, "Christ has many forms of self-manifestation." You wonder if this will do for a theme. You will try to universalize it. One thing you are already sure of. The words "Christ's Many Forms" is a fine subject for a sermon. You have read and studied and meditated. You have prayed. Two words of Scripture, "another form" have become the occasion of a great light to your soul. You have Christ in a fresh perspective. You see Him related savingly to our human predicament. Christ is God taking effective measures to inaugurate and carry through a Divine crusade of redemption. This calls for revelation, for self-manifestation, in one form after another. Christ will not tolerate being put out of business as Saviour of the world. He will see to it that there is always fresh witness, always something coming to light and someone coming to the light, so that it can always be said, "After that He was manifested in another form."

Now for a theme. You write them down without any intended connection. The same thing is said again and again with slight variation. You crave a sentence for the ages, a timeless truth suggested by your text and in harmony with it, which will speak home to the heart of your hearers. Since this is not a cut and dried presentation but a sample demonstration of "bleeding" effort, it may serve as a disclosure of the birth pangs which attend the production of a suitable theme for a sermon on "Christ's Many Forms." Note that the sentences are not a development of the thought of the sermon. They constitute the preparatory struggle before you begin to write the sermon, the quest for a theme. At the risk of seeming repetitious, the detailed efforts to get the necessary theme are given in full and numbered. It is a glimpse into "the preacher's workshop":

1. When Christ finds it necessary to manifest Himself, He can do so in different forms.

2. When Christ finds it necessary, He can manifest Himself in another form than the one to which we have become accustomed and insensitive.

3. When Christ finds it necessary, He manifests Himself in new forms for the sake of His cause.

4. When Christ finds it necessary, He manifests Himself in other forms than those which have become unreal or than those which once served His purpose but are now impotent.

5. Christ appears in new forms when the life has gone out of old forms.

6. Christ appears in new forms when current forms bury Him or hide Him or obscure Him or prove insufficient or have served their purpose or no longer serve.

7. Christ meets the needs of every age by appropriate forms of self-manifestation.

8. Christ knows how to prove the reality of His presence with His people.

9. The living Christ is not limited to one form of manifesting Himself.

10. Christ's appearance in different forms insures the triumphant progress of His work.

11. After Christ seems to be "done for," He shows Himself Master of the situation.

12. Christ uses the necessary techniques to show Himself the living Head of the Church.

13. Christ is always on the job.
14. Christ has a risen, deathless life.
15. Christ has the necessary techniques to produce conviction of the reality of His risen life.
16. Christ inspires fresh testimony by certifying His living presence.
17. Christ appears in other forms when accepted forms no longer do justice to His significance.
18. Christ appears in a different form when conditions call for new inspiration and new methods.
19. Christ appears in different forms as circumstances demand.
20. Christ has what it takes to lead His Church in triumph through all possible circumstances.
21. Christ has what it takes to meet the challenge of every crisis.

Number twenty-one is a sentence of twelve words expressing a permanent, dynamic truth, which seems suitable to serve as a theme. It may serve now to present a tentative outline to be followed by discussion in hope that the reader will feel that he really has been present at the birth of a sermon.

*Subject*: Christ's Many Forms
*Text*: Mark 16:12

*Introduction*:
The shock of Jesus' crucifixion.
Jesus would surely plan to do something about it.
Jesus the Incarnate Son of God would arrange everything.
"After that"—"after these things."
After the betrayal, arrest, trial, crucifixion.
After the bodily form was removed.
After His enemies thought they were rid of Him.

*Theme*: Christ has what it takes to meet the challenge of every crisis.

*Divisions*:
I. The Recurrence of Crisis
   1. Crisis in the Church
      a. The crucifixion
      b. In the subsequent history of the church.

      c. Now in this present time
         World crisis and church crisis
    2. Crisis in personal and family history
       All the ills flesh is heir to.

II. The Sufficiency of Christ

    His many forms: the form of God, etc.
    His eternal being
    (a) His sufficiency in the Church
        Resurrection appearances, Pentecost, Reformation,
        Revivals, new movements such as Missions, Sunday
        School, Salvation Army, Christian Endeavor, Youth
        for Christ, etc.
    (b) His sufficiency in personal and family life. Christ's
        uttermost salvation.

*Conclusion*:

    "O, what a salvation this that Christ liveth in me!"

The conclusion, of course, could strike one of a variety of chords. One idea might be that no one particular form of Christ's self-manifestations exhausts the possibilities. It has been pointed out that the resurrection appearances of our Lord were not in the same form to every one to whom Jesus showed Himself alive. To the two men on the way to Emmaus, the risen Jesus seemed to be a fellow-traveler; to Mary Magdalene, "the gardener," to the disciples after a night of futile fishing, a kindly neighbor who had a breakfast ready for the tired and hungry men. It is also to be remembered that the resurrection of Jesus was not a return to life in the body on our present earthly plane. Jesus stood forth in resurrection life on the other side of death. The body of His earthly life was changed into a spiritual body, raised in incorruption, in glory, in power, thus belonging to another plane of being, to the life of heaven. Hence, the enormous difficulty of people on the earthly plane with all their "blind spots" seeing Him. But the risen Christ was equal to it and the chosen witnesses were Divinely qualified to see Him as risen and alive and manifest. Thus each witness would have his own story, his own personal portrait of the living Christ, showing not that the different resurrection appearances of Christ were illusions, but forms of Christ's self-manifestation suited to the persons who received them. The endeavor has been made to illustrate as follows. Let twelve people, each having the same kind of camera, take a picture of the same landscape. The twelve pictures will all look the same. Now bring on twelve artists with canvas, brush and paint. You will get twelve different interpretations of the same landscape. No one of them paints a false picture. Each paints what he sees and the twelve portraits bring out the glory of the scene according to the artistic insight of each artist. All that they paint is there. Each sees something distinctive. So wonderful is Christ and such is the varied light in which different believers see Him. Therefore, the proper conclusion is: Know Christ for yourself and do not be skeptical when others see what you do not. Pay the price of seeing Christ for yourself and getting even better sight to see Him as He is in all the beauty of His Divine nature and His redemptive love.

In the tentative sermon outline presented, "the shock of Jesus' crucifixion" to His disciples has been suggested as a fitting introduction. The crucifixion is also suggested for consideration in the first division and it might be pointed out that one could hardly use this material in both places. This is true and the proper place to put it would be at the beginning of the first division. The reason you find it in the suggested introduction is because the introduction was written first instead of last. It is best to write the body of a sermon first after final selection has been made of a theme. No one builds a porch before he builds a house. You build the house first after you have made a plan. In sermon construction your plan is your theme. Just as a house comes before a porch, so, in sermon construction, you develop your sermon body first, then the conclusion and then the introduction or porch.

Ideally, every sermon should be written, not in order to be delivered from manuscript, but as an antidote to laziness, as an aid to producing preachers of qualified competence, as a preacher's way of holding himself unswervingly to paying the price of doing mightily the greatest task on earth. When a sermon has been brought by writing to a suitable climax, the preacher will be best prepared properly to introduce it.

In twenty-one tentative themes presented, one read as follows: Christ is always on the job. Cannot that statement do for an idea for the introduction? Christ's resurrection appearances were self-manifestations of Christ in a time of crisis. Christ gave proof that He never lets His people down. He is never defeated. The eternally living Christ is eternally resourceful. Provision is made for every conceivable need of the Church and of Christian individuals and families. Here surely is a pertinent way to introduce the theme that "Christ has what it takes to meet the challenge of every crisis."

Another idea for an introduction might be that the Church or the Christian individual may be down but neither is ever permanently out. Both church and individual Christian are forever solvent because Christianity is a living religion and the Christ Who lives forever guarantees the perpetual security of His cause and people. When a preacher has gotten a real theme and has written the body and conclusion of his sermon, he can qualify as an expert porch-builder, that is to say, he has gotten to a point where introductions come in like a flood.

It has been suggested that when a preacher gets a satis-factory theme worked out, he has the plan which determines the structure of the sermon. It must be stressed that the sermon is not really and fully born until the sermon body with proper conclusion and introduction has been written out in full. A thematic Christian sermon is a living organism, but there is no such thing as a living organism without a body. It cannot be satisfactory from any ideal standpoint to have a sermon body only in mind. It may be quite a real body before Sunday, possibly also on Sunday, but it will not likely continue to live as a written skeleton. Many a minister has preached one of these "old" skeletal sermons in another pulpit during his vacation, only to discover to his frustration that the "bones" did not live, that he was not getting the joy out of it which he got when he preached it in his own pulpit and that he was not putting it over like he did when he first preached it. If for no other reason than to keep his own nose on the grindstone in the interest of his personal competence, a minister must hold himself as without excuse unless he sees his sermons through to a written finish. If even for the best of reasons this is again and again impossible, a preacher must judge himself as then having in so far fallen short of the ideal.

At times the more advanced nations of the world must fight to retain man's inalienable rights and to keep the devils of sinister greed and passion from lording it over humanity with conscienceless savagery. In such a crisis the price in blood and struggle and treasure must be paid. The prosecution of a world war is a stupendous, colossal, astonishing performance. A like performance must be the enterprise to change man the rebel, into a friend of God and humanity. It takes all any preacher has. It takes all any Christian has. Preaching the Gospel of Christ is the supreme, Divinely ordained and honored technique for overcoming the barriers of human resistance. Only the highest possible ideals of preaching, laboriously and prayerfully pursued, with never a let-up or a let-down, can match the hour of responsibility and opportunity to gain Christ His crown in a world "hell-bent for destruction." Shun self-pity, slough off the robes of laziness, shunt away soft and easy aids; live, sweat, struggle, bleed and die to preach with earned, home-grown, God-given ability the glad tidings of redemption and the solemn alarms of coming and present doom to the impenitent.

As to the body of a thematic Christian sermon, the outline presented on "Christ's Many Forms" affords occasion to discuss a matter of supreme importance from the structural angle. If the sermon body is to be a balanced and progressive development of the essential thought of the theme, the strictest care must be given to stick to the thought of a division when that particular division is being presented and developed. The preacher must be on his guard lest he introduce the material of Division II into Division I. It is the most natural thing in the world for a preacher to anticipate, thus eliminating the important element of surprise and, therefore, depriving the sermon of its power to hold the attention of the hearers.

To illustrate: Division I is rhetorically named "The Recurrence of Crisis." A logical statement ought to follow this like the following: "The life of the Church and the life of an individual Christian always face the threat of events which give the lie to faith." Then would follow the development of that idea. Allusion would first be made, quite naturally, to the shock of the crucifixion to the followers of Jesus. Effort must be expended to make it clear and real how awful it was that one such as Jesus came to such an end of His earthly life and ministry. You picture what a crisis it was for Jesus' followers thus to be deprived of Jesus. This terrible experience of theirs is to be typical of other crises in other times and lives, some of which are also to be realistically portrayed. The preacher must under no circumstances at this point, that is, in the first division of the sermon, introduce the relief which came to these believers by Christ appearing to them in "another form." To do that would rob the rest of the sermon of the progress and climax which every sermon must have. Division I must deal only with crisis and what crisis does to Christian faith.

How natural it would be for a preacher to picture the despair of the disciples and then go on immediately to proclaim that Jesus showed Himself alive to them. The sermon would then become a collection of illustrations. The hearers would appreciate the first one, but it is a question whether they would be carried along with breathless interest with such a form of presentation. To follow statement of one crisis with statement of its relief and keep on alternating between crisis and relief, is to tell the same thing over and over again. To stick to the matter of crisis in Division I is to make Division I a realistic portrayal of one great aspect of life which calls for remedy and solution. People will be asking, "What are you going to do about it?" and when you announce as your second division "The Sufficiency of Christ" the congregation will be keyed up to hear your presentation of Christ's many forms of self-manifestation as demonstrating His competence and sufficiency for every conceivable crisis. In Division II you are done with description of "the dark night of the soul." You are in the realm of Christ's conquering grace, of His will and power to see His people through. Allusion to crises presented in Division I is of course in order in Divison II as introducing other forms of Christ's self-manifestation, but descriptive power in Division II is confined to Christ's sufficiency as it was in Division I to the reality and devastation of crisis. Division I shows with gathering momentum what happens and its blighting effects. Division II goes deeper and deeper into the Remedy, portraying the living Christ as making His people more than conquerors by self-disclosures of His presence and saving power. A sermon on "Christ's Many Forms" as outlined sets up the background in Division I for a real preaching in Division II of the Christ Who never fails. Perhaps already you have thought of another conclusion. Your soul is singing, "When I fear my faith will fail, Christ will hold me fast." You are planning to have that sung as a solo number after your sermon, the congregation joining in the chorus. Great preaching gives God's people great times.

# VIII

## Selection in Thematic Sermon Construction

A PREACHER should never allow himself to get "preached-out." An effective barrier to such a condition is thematic Christian preaching based on unremitting faithfulness in scholarly all-around preparation. As sure as a preacher with the necessary intellectual apparatus pays the price of adequate study, he is sure to experience "an embarrassment of riches." For such a glad hour there is a principle of selection calculated to save the day. Selection is always in the interest of unity. The grandest idea may have to be laid by in store instead of being used in the sermon under preparation. You may not want to file it or scrap it. It grips you. But so do this and that and other facts and ideas. Make up your mind, sir. A sermon is not a "string of sausages" nor an untracked forest with ideas as trees and the trees so thick and numberless that you cannot see or chop your way through. A sermon is a unity, an integer, an integrated whole, a living organism, a shining highway to and from God. You will have to borrow familiar words from the apostle Paul and make them a slogan in every sermon: "This one thing I do."

How can a preacher bring himself to the happy point and moment when an embarrassment of riches in gathered sermon material makes it imperative to apply the principle of selection? The Scripture discussed in the previous chapter will serve to show how this comes about. "And after these things he was manifested in another form unto two of them as they walked into the country." The words "another form" suggested: first, other forms of Christ's self-manifestation and, secondly, other forms of Christ's existence. Almost at once the preacher is face to face with Christ as an eternal Being and the variety

of Christ's possible forms of existence and self-manifestation.
Here is a possible sermon on the Person of Christ, a doctrinal
sermon on the Person of Christ, perhaps a doctrinal sermon
on the Person and Work of Christ, because you get to see that
the forms of Christ's self-manifestation are definitely related
to Christ's work as the Saviour of the world.   You get back
to your text. You ask questions, giving thought to the words
"another form." What was this form in which Christ now
manifested Himself? How does this resurrection form differ
from other forms? Why was this particular form of self-manifestation necessary? What was the need and occasion of this
particular form? How effective was it? What other forms of
self-manifestation were there before this one? Will there be
other forms later? What was the purpose of other forms of
Christ's self-manifestation? What reasons and purposes guarantee other forms of future disclosure? Here is a vast continent of revealed truth, relevant to human interest and need,
pertinent to God's self-revelation and man's redemption, vastly
more than enough for a single, simple, powerful sermon. Right
in this single area of the Person and Work of Christ, the
principles of selection must become operative as well as the
principles of unity, progress, balance, symmetry, purpose and
goal.

The words of the text, together with the context, certainly
justify taking the words "And after these things" as including
what happened to Jesus as indicated by His arrest, trial, condemnation and crucifixion. Suddenly it occurs to you that
what was done to Jesus was done by the ecclesiastical authorities, that is to say, by the Church. You recall how it was expressed in a book you read, "The God Whom they worshipped
came to His temple and was crucified by His worshippers."
You are repeating to yourself the familiar words, "He came
unto His own and His own received Him not." You are
aware that another vast continent of facts is now opened. Subjects for another type of sermon are brewing. "What the
Church Did To Christ" is an initial form of a possible sermon
topic. Later you have clearer light and you have made up your

mind to preach a sermon on the arresting question, "Will the Church destroy Christianity?" You may possibly, perhaps very likely, find a different Scripture verse for it, but the idea came to you while preparing to preach on Mark 16:12. In your work of preparation, it flashed in on you that it was the Church which rejected and crucified Jesus. You naturally expected to bring it into your sermon on Christ's many forms, but you make up your mind that this matter of an apostate church is something of enormous proportions all by itself. Moreover, you have so much already to preach now in the field of the Person and Work of Christ that it becomes clear that there is vastly more than you will be able to handle in one sermon. Here is where the value of thematic preaching comes in, as also the beneficent tyranny of the principle of selection. A preacher can kill a sermon by overloading it with truth and facts pertinent and relevant enough to the great field of a particular Scripture verse or passage, but Scripture truth is not something you can gulp down in big chunks without mastication. There is never any use of preaching unless what you say "lives and moves and has being" while you preach, giving the hearers the impression, experience and realization of its reality and power. A preacher cannot jam it in and ram it down. Something to live by has to be taken in gradually in harmony with principles and processes of spiritual appropriation, assimilation and digestion. Therefore you give the people sermons like meals, vitamin measured, with calories calculated and satisfaction guaranteed. Sermons with themes and which ring the changes on a definite theme, constitute the technique for such nutritive preaching.

In the study of Mark 16:12, a point is now reached where the preacher has already the raw material of two good sermons; one on "Christ's Many Forms" in the doctrinal sphere of Christ's Person and Work, and a second on "Will the Church Destroy Christianity?" The latter is also in the field of doctrine, having to do with the doctrine of the Church. The idea of what the Church did to Christ suggests the idea of an apostate church. You sit back to ponder the matter. You have studied Sacred History, by which you understand Bible history, including Old Testament history, New Testament history, and Inter-Testament history. You have also studied the history of the Christian Church from apostolic times down. It comes to you that backsliding has marked the church in all ages. There is no such thing as a permanent status quo of realized salvation in the history of God's people on earth. Remember now that our present discussion is from the sermonic standpoint, from the angle of what to preach and why. What the established Church of Jesus' day did to Jesus directs your attention to the behaviour of the Church as such in all ages. Included in it, of course, is the whole field of general Christian behaviour, to which you mean to give thought in due time, but just now you face the terrible things done by the church officially from age to age, the apostasy, the progressive apostasy which marks the history of official Judaism and Christianity. You may ask, "Why preach on the apostasy of the Church?" "What purpose of a redemptive character can be served by airing the Church's apostasy?" It ought to be evident that with such fatal drifts operative in organized religion, it is always high time to erect barriers against this sinister tendency and by pertinent thematic Bible preaching induce Christians to make conscience of their consecration and of seeing to it that they keep consciously and constantly rejoicing in the Lord.

The Holy Spirit gives timely aid to preachers who bleed to do their work as it should be done. You now are grappling with the idea of an apostate Church, grappling with it from the preaching end, from the standpoint of your duty as a watchman on the walls of Zion. You open your Bible and before you is the book of Isaiah, chapter I. "Hear, O heavens, and give ear, O earth: for Jehovah hath spoken: I have nourished and brought up children, and they have rebelled against me. The ox knoweth his owner, and the ass his master's crib, but Israel doth not know, my people doth not consider." Here is a marvelously realistic picture of defection on the part of God's people. It is represented as a ground for astonishment throughout the universe that a people for whom God had done so much should fall even below animals by their ill-considered ungrateful behaviour. Here is human behaviour set in the light of God's practical lovingkindness. How contemporaneous! What a sermon it will be when you have done what is necessary to get it ready! What a lofty realism will be in it! How you will ring the changes on God's appeal to reason, "Come, now and let us reason together, saith Jehovah, etc." "God's Appeal to Man's Reason" already sounds like a fine sermon subject. Imagine landing in Isaiah I by way of Mark 16:12, which suggested to your mind the idea of an apostate church because of what the Church did to Jesus.

It may be only the morning after when you are reading in the Book of Revelation, chapter III. You stop after you read verse twenty. "Behold, I stand at the door and knock: if any man hear my voice and open the door, I will come in to him and will sup with him, and he with me." You have always associated this verse with an evangelistic sermon and understood it to represent Christ as knocking at the door of the heart of the unsaved in hope of being admitted. Today it comes to you that this verse is part of a message written to a church and that in reality Christ is here represented as being outside of His church, as standing on the outside of His own church, standing at the door of His church and seeking to be admitted. You wonder how Christ got out of that church. You may be sure He was put out or forced out by the unchristian behaviour of those on the inside. It is possible that He went out because He could not stand for what was going on inside. But He wants to get back. It is His church. His expressed purpose is, "I will build my church." But here He is outside of His own church, either definitely put out or unwillingly forced out by conditions out of harmony with His significance and presence. Christ is trying to get into His own church. It must be an apostate church where the door of a church is barred against the Christ Whose church it is. You now have New Testament corroboration of the fatal drift toward apostasy which marks the age-long history of God's Church on earth. You began, you remember, with Mark 16:12. God graciously rewarded toil and answered prayer by giving you a sermon on "Christ's Many Forms." But the Lord added an embarrassment of riches as it was opened to you what the Church did to Jesus. Presently you had another sermon in the incubator on "Will the Church Destroy Christianity?" You were led into Isaiah I and to another prospective sermon on "God's Appeal to Reason." Another flash led you to the book of Revelation and to a sermon on "Christ At The Door Of His Church." All this as a result of following God's Providential lead in studying Mark 16:12.

The possibilities of sermonic enrichment through becoming a thematic preacher are endless. Your work on Bible verses and passages becomes a studious inquiry for essential, timeless, pertinent contemporary truth. When discovered, the struggle is on for a theme, some form of expression which will make the truth like a polished shaft or a lustrous diamond. When you get the theme you want, you have the plan, the goal, the purpose, the direction for the sermon. The principle of selection now takes the controls. The theme rules out much as at present not of major relevance. The theme has priority. Only the directly relevant gets shared priority. Thus sermonic riches increase. The three additional sermons already in hand as well as the one for next Sunday are still only a part of constantly increasing wealth.

It is difficult to keep confining your thought to Mark 16:12 without taking in verse 13, "And they went away and told it unto the rest: neither believed they them." You learn that not only are there fatal drifts and sinister tendencies toward apostasy operative in the Christian Church and in the Christian life, but also a growing inclination to unbelief in the presence of spiritual realities. Secular idealism invades the realm of God, the inner light grows dim, fellowship with Christ wanes, the reality of the unseen recedes, the far horizons of the soul contract, the form of godliness persists without the power, things Christian become drab, alleged emotionalism in the Christian life is decried, insistence is on the "scientific" attitude and final virtual unbelief assumes prerogatives of Judge of all spiritual adventures and attainments. Here is another field for sermonic exploration. Already the preacher's mind is impressed with the Perils and Penalties of Unbelief and he confronts another world of reality which no thematic Christian preacher dare ignore.

The preacher may well ask, "Why did those early friends of Jesus disbelieve the testimony of other friends of Jesus who witnessed that they saw Jesus alive?" It may be asked, "Why did those friends of Jesus who refused to accept the testimony of others, themselves miss the blessing of seeing the risen Lord?" This suggests the case of Thomas which is given in Scripture for the instruction of the Church. It is well to go into it how one can be in on any fresh self-manifestation of the living, reigning Christ. Thomas missed it because he absented himself from the place and time of Christ's self-manifestation. But he was personally let in on it in due time. The question is important: What is the secret of Christian vision? It cannot be denied that the craving for fresh, first-hand, personal Christian experience is legitimate. God means every soul to have it. The intention of testimony is to inspire personal quest. Grand as Pentecost was, each wants it for himself. God means him to have it. The chances are it is one's own fault if he does not get it as soon as others. Would that all God's people were prophets and all mankind God's people! The preaching possibilities of all this are evident. The start was made from Mark 16:12. See how far we have travelled. You study faithfully and deeply one verse or passage of Scripture. You get facts, truths, flashes, inspirations, insights, understanding enough for six to a dozen sermons. You cannot begin to convey it all in one sermon. You are not a wholesaler in distribution even though God shoots it in to you on a large scale. Moreover, the people cannot take it in. A doctor prescribed one sixtieth of a grain of arsenic for a patient to be taken at stated intervals. He poured these tiny tablets into a little bottle from a big bottle. He spilled some on the floor. The patient's pet dog lapped up these very tiny tablets as if they were candy. In due time the dog blew up and died.

No such effort would follow swallowing the Word of God in large doses, but the point is, that there is a proper amount for a single sermon adjusted to capacity to assimilate. A thematic Christian sermon is a technique for the measurable nourishment of God's people with bread from heaven and for bringing back to life famished souls in the far country of sin. Capacity to assimilate the Word of God varies, but even the largest eater here is well-fed by a real thematic sermon. If he is well-developed in power of spiritual digestion, he can do some thinking on his own account. Preaching is not intended to do the thinking of God's people. It is intended to inspire them to think. Your technique of thematic sermon construction may well be divulged to your people in hope that they will read the Word with a more inquiring mind. Teach your people to ask questions of the Word as they read. It is a simple, wholesome device for getting more out of it. But the preacher with personal stocks of Bible knowledge mounting apace will adhere to thematic quest and thematic sermon structure, laying foundations so that he will not be preached out if his first pastorate proves to be his only pastorate and God spares him to hold it for forty years. When God's preachers are truly God's prophets they qualify as life-guides for a lifetime. The principle of selection makes excellent thematic preachers and becomes an exquisite art. It develops a fine sense of the relevant, enabling a preacher to ration ideas and illustrations, establish priorities and apply constantly increasing intelligence to pointed, polished and powerful thematic sermon construction.

When a preacher means business in sermon preparation, construction and delivery, determined not to make the minds and hearts of his people a dumping ground for anything he happens to think of or to have read, his preaching becomes expansive and comprehensive as well as highly concentrated. The concentration appears in each thematic sermon, the expansion and comprehension in the widening range of subjects in reserve and sure to appear in due time in thematic sermon form. Let this further illustration on the results of studying Mark

16:12 serve. Christ's many forms brought to mind such a verse as I Cor. 12:27, "Now ye are the body of Christ, and severally members thereof." The teaching is seen to be that Christ's present form of self-manifestation is the Church and every individual Christian. Your knowledge of Pentecost teaches that the Holy Spirit is God's promised technique for making Christ a living presence in the heart of every believer. The conception of the Church as Christ's body and of individual Christians as severally members of the body of Christ brings understanding of how important to Christ the Church and the individual Christian are. If in any given generation the Church is moved by the world's indifference to a sense of frustration and futility or individual ministers and laymen are disposed to discouragement by the way things are going in the local church and community, as well as generally, what a source of revival it is to the drooping spirit to recall how significant to Christ His Church and people are. A hard-beset preacher might possibly be inclined to ask, "Does the Church Matter?" Blessed is such a preacher if the Holy Spirit brings I Cor. 12:27 to his mind. The Holy Spirit did just that in studying Christ's many forms. To the embarrassment of riches which came in like a flood is now added this sermon topic, "Does the Church Matter?" and its text, I Cor. 12:27.

You cannot preach on everything at once nor say everything in one sermon. But that is no reason why you should not take stock and adopt a resolution of conservation, not for reasons mechanical, but for vital reasons, in hope, that is, that all the truths which gripped you in your thematic quest in the field of a selected text, may be assimilated and transfigured into intellectual and spiritual background. Since these chapters illustrate a method and its harvest, this is how it sizes up at present. The following brand-new, original sermons are to be seen through to a triumphant finish: I: Christ's Many Forms, Mark 16:12. II. Will the Church Destroy Christianity? Luke 23:33. III. God's Appeal to Reason, Isaiah 1:18. IV. Christ At the Door, Rev. 3:20. V. Does the Church Matter? I Cor. 12:27. VI. The Perils or Penalty of

Unbelief, Luke 1:20. VII. The Secret of Christian Vision, Matt. 5:8 or John 20:24. The suggested texts for the six extra sermons God gave you in studying Mark 16:12 are of course suggestions only, indicating new fields of study and further trials of spiritual adventure and discovery.

Said one, "I get more out of it when our pastor talks to the children than I do out of his regular sermons." "What's wrong with his sermons?" said the other. "O, our minister just rambles," was the answer. What preacher wants to be "a rambling rake of poverty" or even just a rambler? The Bible is the world's greatest gold mine. All preachers and all the rest of God's people are challenged to become "gold-diggers" in a lofty, noble sense, digging in the spacious mines of God's self-revelation, for the pure gold of redemptive truth. The more of this gold you dig out, the greater will be your value to human society. The gold of God's grace is social as well as individual. Preachers are ordained to give mankind God's gold and to lure the world to go in for gold digging in God's gold mine. "The blessing of the Lord, it maketh rich and addeth no sorrow thereto." Is this another sermon floating in? "Breathe on us, breath of God."

# IX

# Thematic Expository Preaching

THE possibilities of thematic Christian preaching have effective demonstration in the field of expository preaching. Imagine preaching a sermon with the entire eighth chapter of Paul's Epistle to the Romans as the text! How can the wealth of Christian truth in that chapter conceivably be condensed into an intelligible, living, helpful sermon requiring twenty-five or thirty minutes to deliver? We shall see. One thing is certain. Only a thematic Christian preacher can undertake it with any hope of success. When a minister substitutes a running commentary for a sermon on Romans 8, he is virtually compelled to read the verses on which he proposes to comment as a part of the sermon. This compels him, in the case of Romans 8, to read publicly in sermon time a matter of thirty-nine verses. Very little time would be left for proposed comment. The preacher would have to turn grasshopper, jumping from verse to verse, inviting his hearers to jump with him. As has been said, if he felt persecuted in one verse, he would flee promptly into another. It would be like taking a jet-plane at five hundred miles an hour through a wonderland of scenic beauty and expecting the people to gain a due impression of the wonders of nature. It just cannot be done.

If preparation for a thematic sermon on Romans 8 leads you to study Hodge's *Commentary on Romans,* you will learn that the chapter presents seven reasons why a Christian is secure. That captures your attention. You are hearing plenty every day about social security and other brands of the same commodity. Surely the words "Christian Security" impress you at once as a promising topic. Hodge's suggestiveness might even induce you to take as topic, "Seven Reasons For

Christian Security." Precedent for such a topic was given when a foremost preacher announced as topic of next Sunday's sermon, "Seven Ways In Which A Modern Man Can Pray." You will hold the matter in abeyance because somehow, if possible, you would like to have Christ even in your sermon topics. Your further sermon preparation is showing you that according to Romans 8 a Christian is eternally secure. You are already constructing theme sentences and you already have it down that "one who puts his trust in Christ is forever safe in Him." In case your finally selected theme is the one just written, you may choose as your topic, not, "Christian Security" but "Safe In Christ." You never miss a chance to give Christ priority in topic, theme and sermon. Your one object as preacher and Christian is to exalt your Lord and Saviour by lip and life, to lift Christ up in sermon and service.

The idea of being "safe in Christ" brings to mind the hymn, "Safe in the arms of Jesus." This lures you to your hymn book. You are looking for and finding any number of hymns on Christian security: "Rock of ages, cleft for me," "In the secret of His presence," "O safe to the Rock that is higher than I," "The Lord's our Rock, in Him we hide," "He will hide me," etc. Your session with your hymn book becomes a time of revelation to you. You make up your mind to make more use of your hymn book in sermon preparation from now on. Golden sentences leap up at you holding promise of serving as themes with due credit. You gain a new awareness of the preciousness of Christ as well as of His grace and glory. These hymns are talking to you, "deep calling unto deep." They not only touch the heart; they enlighten your mind. A new interest is awakened in you to explore the field of hymnology, to specialize on hymns of salvation which glorify the Saviour and to become more familiar with the hymns which preach the many-sided, universal Christ. Not only do you feel fresh impetus to preach Christ more than ever but to have it sung by means of these simple Gospel hymns. You have suddenly become more aware of your responsibility for the music of the sanctuary. It occurs to you that a simple Gospel hymn, properly interpreted by a member of your church choir, who is a Christian, may be used of God to win souls for Christ and do far more good than some anthems which seem to be little more than exercises in vocal gymnastics. No, no, no, you are not against the singing of the great anthems of the church. But it will do no harm to confer with the proper persons about the music of the church, to tell them lovingly of your spiritual aims, to secure cooperation in crowning and preaching Christ in all the music of the church. One thing you are absolutely sure of and that is that you propose to make your church more and more a singing church and that what is sung will be the music of the Gospel. You will pay the price of becoming a competent thematic expounder of the Word of God and you intend to have it sung also, so help you God.

You are quite at ease, now, about your forthcoming sermon on Romans 8. Topic and theme give cue to what the chapter is about. Only that in the chapter which is relevant to the idea of Christian security and being forever safe in Christ can have a place in the sermon. The more you think of it the more aware you become that the whole chapter has to do with the eternal security of the Christian. How are you going to handle it all? When you announce that you have selected the entire eighth chapter of Paul's letter to the Romans as the basis of the sermon, you cannot be expected to read it all, because it would take too much time. What then is the best thing to do? See if the chapter contains a verse, a clause or question which might be called a key verse or clause or question. In Romans 8 more than one verse may meet the requirements but you must limit yourself to one. In Romans 8 the key verse may very well be verse 35 and specifically the question which introduces the verse: "Who shall separate us from the love of Christ?" Let us suppose that you take as subject, "Christian Security." A proper way to begin the sermon would be as follows: The subject of the sermon is "Christian Security" based on the entire eighth chapter of Paul's letter to the Romans. If one were asked to suggest a key-verse of this chapter for the message of the hour, the answer could well be in terms of the question which introduces the thirty-fifth verse, "Who shall separate us from the love of Christ?" etc. Then would follow the usual introduction closing with statement of theme and divisions after which would come the body of the sermon and the conclusion. One caution is necessary. Be sure to say "key-verse" or "key-sentence" or "key question" when starting an expository sermon. Do not call the key-verse the text of the sermon. When expounding in sermonic form a portion of Scripture, the entire portion is the text. You are not basing your sermon on a key-verse. The key-verse is offered as a possible memory verse for the congregation. The idea of a key-verse, key-sentence or key-question is thematic pointedness, impressing the listener with the specific definiteness of the preacher's ministry on this particular occasion. Every sermon is a shot at a target. Put Romans 8 into one sermon. If you do it thematically you have an atomic bomb. The spiritual powers of the universe are latent in the Word of God. Preachers must match scientists in constructing atomic bombs of regenerating grace so that the world will become more and more aware that it cannot hold out against God's saving might in Christ. A thematic Christian expository sermon splits open atomic redemptive truths and liberates forces which mean the salvation of mankind. What such chemicals as uranium and barium are to the construction of atomic bombs, that God's regenerating, justifying and sanctifying grace in Christ Jesus are to the bursting bombs of thematic expository Christian sermons. Let no preacher fail to specialize on Pentecost, the Holy Spirit, the joy of salvation, the Person and Work of Christ and the coming Kingdom of God so that the moral and spiritual giant forces of the universe can operate through his weakness to achieve the results of omnipotence.

If the principle of selection is to be operative in the quest of the right sermon theme, it continues on duty when handling the details of chapter or portion in thematic expository preaching. If you preach on a somewhat long verse of Scripture you may be able to explain all the details of your text

in relation to your sermon theme.  That is one way of handling details.  You take them up one by one and open the heart
of each.  That cannot be done with a long passage like Romans
8.  Two further courses are open.  You can pick and choose
among the details and select certain details for full exposition, the given exposition being a sample of what is char-
acteristic of the others.  You select certain details because of
their possible greater relevance to contemporaneous matters
or because they fit better into your local church situation,
although what was said in a previous chapter about preaching
to humanity is not to be forgotten.  It is very much subject
to doubt whether God ever calls on a preacher to call down a
particular individual in a sermon in public worship.  Church
discipline furnishes the cue to such a situation.  Keeping an
eye on your theme, details may be selected out of a larger
number which more specifically and clearly lend themselves
to the progressive and unified exposition of the theme.

A third way of treating details is to mass their significance
into one interpretive exposition.  You look for the total meaning, the general, timeless, universal significance, the cosmic,
redemptive import and strength of all the details in their combined yield and you expound it to humanity and the ages.
What an immortalizing experience it is to become a systematic,
thematic, expounder of the Word of God.  The basic, cosmic,
redemptive forces inherent in God's Word do their constructive
work in the soul of the preacher, begetting a sense of authority
which God intends His servants to have when their feet are
planted on the Rock of Ages and they go by what God says.
The closer a preacher lives to God, the more power he has.
The more he lives by every word that cometh out of the
mouth of God, the more use God will make of him.  He may
have a thorn in the flesh like Paul did, be it sore eyes, a
weak presence, inability to speak with eloquence or even epi-
leptic fits, as some claim, but God will take that weak, devoted
servant of His and make him mighty to the pulling down of
strongholds.  David Brainerd, that Christlike missionary to
the American Indians, languished in bed with consumption,

but when the hour for preaching came, he preached for an hour and a half through power divine. John Wesley rode twenty-six thousand miles on horseback, preaching sermons from twenty minutes to three hours long. He travelled and preached for half a century after the real light of God came to him at thirty-five. George Whitefield was dying on his feet but he preached with atomic, that is to say, Pentecostal force. Do not worry about details or about personal weakness. The Christ who lives in the power of an endless life has His home in the heart of every consecrated preacher and the Holy Spirit is there, too, to make Christ an experienced reality. You can do all things in Christ Who gives you strength. Go in for what God says. Study the Word. The Word of God is a thematic Word. The scarlet thread of sacrifice runs through it. The blood of God's sacrifice in Christ drenches its pages. Redemption is the theme-song. "Unto him that loveth us, and loosed us from our sins by his blood; and he made us to be a kingdom, and to be priests unto his God and Father; to him be the glory and the dominion forever and ever. Amen."

A thematic expository sermon treats only so much of the truth of a passage of Scripture as is contributory to the theme. In the sermon case under discussion, Romans 8 furnishes the theme and the theme determines what teachings of the chapter are to be embodied in the sermon. A thematic sermon on a chapter like Romans 8 is like a streamlined train speeding across a vast continent of Christian truth to a Grand Central station called Personal Security. The track is laid on the verses and facts pertinent to the chosen theme of Christian Security. If all the verses and facts are seen to bear on the topic and theme chosen, the sermon must make it clear. It is best, then, in the case of such a long chapter, to mass details, to interpret their broad, essential, fundamental significance and relation to the theme. It would be impossible to explain all the relevant details. To select some details for treatment and omit others is possible and legitimate, but you will have to weigh the matter and decide which method of handling details does fullest justice to the chapter and to the unified exposition of the theme. There is no intention in this discussion of stressing a mechanical process. It is entirely a matter of the preacher doing justice to the Word of God, to his congregation and to his own task. No halter of legality is laid upon a preacher. The effort is to remove halters of aimlessness, slovenliness, laziness, and ignorance or to prevent their being imposed. The purpose is to contribute to the creation of a new and higher grade of preachers and preaching, to help to inaugurate under God a new era of pulpit ministry to our human predicament, to say what by God's Spirit might prove a word in season for the production of prophetic, apostolic, Pentecostal preachers of God's freely offered grace in Christ. One of the masked perils of the Christian ministry is that a minister does not have to punch a time-clock. Domestic inducement may be pressing to function as chief cook and bottle-washer and to lend a hand at housework, but Christian conscience must triumph and hold a preacher to his immense office. While God's servant is busy here and there where he has no business either to be busy or to be, he flounders around in a sea of futilities, "while Rome burns," with no developing technique to stop the forces of moral destruction.

It is conceivable that a preacher who studies a chapter like Romans 8 might want to preach a separate sermon on each of the seven reasons for Christian security. It might be very well done, very worth doing and prove profitable. But, generally speaking, it is not wise to keep striking one chord too continuously on successive occasions. Give seven Sundays to one subject and people will get tired of it. Some will say, "Is that one thing all he knows?" Moreover, no pastorate is a hundred years long and the manifold wisdom enshrined in God's Word calls for covering wide open spaces of revelation. In preaching and in listening to sermons, "variety is the spice of life." A thematic expository sermon on Romans 8 tells those who are interested that there are seven reasons for Christian Security. It gives the congregation the facts and the feeling of the facts. One who wants to go deeper into it knows how to find the chapter and can read it over and over until it has soaked in "good and plenty." If you keep on one line too long in conversation, it becomes wearisome. A hymn speaks of God's Word as a garden. There is an abundance of trees and fruit. Who wants to stay up in one tree too long?

No preacher should get the idea that he cannot use the same text again in the same pulpit when he has once preached on it. Take the case of Romans 8, for example. Is that chapter to be condemned to disuse because it was used once? Choice verses compose that chapter. Single verses or this or that paragraph may afford substance for subsequent thematic sermons of highly informative and inspirational value. These "single" sermons will be on topics and themes appropriate to the essential meaning of the verse or paragraph selected. A passage of Scripture has more than a primary meaning. It has subordinate teachings. The subordinate teachings have primary significance on special occasions as well as subordinate relevance on all occasions. If nothing that is human is alien to a true Christian minister, nothing that is Divine can be without importance. He will keep studying the Scriptures, knowing that no one has yet exhausted its riches, studying in hope of fresh insights and new experiences of its power.

It is necessary to give a demonstration of thematic expository sermon construction. A sermon on Romans 8 is presented to illustrate procedure in this type of preaching. No teacher of preaching is himself a perfect model. A man who bragged about his wife's calling him a "model" husband was told to look up the word "model" in the dictionary. This was the definition of "model" he found: "a small representation of the real thing." However small the representation, "the real thing" in thematic expository preaching must have some form of representation. See if the principles presented are followed. Is the sermon a unity? Is there progress, balance, symmetry? Is the sermon a thrust? Is it Christian, constructive, contemporaneous? Is it clear enough? Is it true to God's Word? Does it minister to human need? Will it prove bread from heaven to hearts which hunger for security? Can a preacher be a failure who every Sunday presents sermons of such substance? These are vital questions. Ask them about your own sermons. Put yourself on the carpet. How does your preaching stand up under cross-examination?

## X

# Thematic Topical Preaching — Usual Form

A TOPICAL sermon is the development in sermonic form of a Bible truth. At a time when it was usual always to choose a "text" from Scripture for every sermon, a topical sermon was defined as one which developed a teaching or deduction drawn from a Bible verse or passage without limiting the development to the directions indicated by the verse or passage. The preacher got an idea for a sermon from some particular verse or passage and then he went his own sermonic way. His sermonic way was usually Biblical but not thematic. Such is the power of the Word of God that a topical sermon can be very powerful as long as it is Biblical, even if it is not thematic.

As long as preaching is Biblical, God will honor the preacher by using the preaching as the channel of His saving grace. The thematic form of sermonic Bible preaching is a sure-fire technique for putting the truth of God over to the mind and heart of the congregation. Why "scrap" text and technique in the interest of a less effective variety? One famous preacher, who apparently does not feel it necessary or wise to begin a sermon with a text, or to develop it thematically, often begins a sermon with a quotation from Carlyle or Ruskin or Emerson or a recent book. No one will shoot him for that, but why should Moses or Isaiah or Paul or even Christ Himself be eliminated from definite preliminary announcement in the interest of variety? That does not make sense. Is one a Bible worshiper because he insists on being a Bible preacher even to the extent of taking a text and sticking to it? The irrelevance of a Christian pulpit to world life and struggle is not due to the supposed monotony of choosing, announcing and expounding a Bible text, but to the substitution of what the apostle Paul calls "the wisdom of the world" for what the same apostle refers to as "the foolishness of God," by which he means the testimony of Christ. When a preacher is brilliant and is pastor of a "swell" church, he will be constantly tempted to place more emphasis on rhetoric than redemption.

But facts are facts and truth is truth. It must be owned that topical preaching is God-honored and God-used preaching if it is Biblical, no matter how poor or fine the rhetoric, whether the sermon be all dolled up in prim and stately style or just a rag doll, even if no text is chosen and no sermonic and thematic development is given to the Biblical topic. A preacher who proclaims what God's Word teaches, who is conscious of heralding a Divine Redeemer and offering a free, supernatural salvation, and who retains the true sense of what he is in the pulpit for, will be used, honored of God and effective.

Topical Bible preaching, with or without a text, is the typical American way of preaching, not exclusively so, but quite generally. Choose a topic, preferably from a definite Bible verse or passage even if you mean to say "goodbye" to it as far as sermon divisions are concerned. Choose a topic but condense and concentrate the results of prayerful study and thought into a theme. Work like a slave on your theme, that is, like a bondservant of Jesus Christ and Christ's freeman, free from mental sloth and pride of intellect. Do your best to have a target and to shoot at it, treading appointed and pointed way to sound the high-calling of God in Christ Jesus.

A college student back in 1903 heard John R. Mott preach a topical sermon at the Northfield Student Conference. For over forty years this sermon has lived in memory and exercised influence in life. The text was James 1:15, "and the sin, when it is full grown, bringeth forth death." The topic was, "The Power of Sin." The theme was that sin is progressively ruinous and finally a fatal power. The sermon had six divisions, each an aspect of the theme, each revealing with cumulative effect the power of sin. I. Its deceiving power. II. Its self-betraying power. III. Its separating power. IV. Its enslaving power. V. Its propagating power. VI. Its deadening power. The preacher got the idea for the sermon as well as his last division from his text. For the rest, he traversed Scripture for his other divisions. It was a topical sermon. No one could miss the theme of that sermon nor escape its tremendous impact. It was mighty. Life for over forty years since has been an astonishing commentary on that sermon for that one student who became a preacher. He has preached that sermon in terms of his own knowledge and experience of life again and again, using the six points and giving due credit. Other students who heard Mott in 1903 or his deeply moved student hearer after he became a preacher have also preached it with the same text and divisions and all testify to its profound impression on preachers and laity alike. It surely is like the splitting of an atomic bomb when a Biblical preacher preaches thematically.

One of the weaknesses of topical preaching is the danger inherent in it of getting away from the Bible. A topical preacher is apt to preach more and more on topics of the day. Such topics may be called problems. The topical preacher is tempted to become a problem preacher. Problem preaching may become like a doctor making a neurotic of some sort the subject of a lecture to an audience which does not have any such malady. It is not commensurate with the scope of Biblical revelation or with the variety of congregational needs as represented by children, youth, adults and aged. Problem preaching can be very useful to many, but it stresses adjustment far more than it does redemption and prescribes technique rather than life-union with Jesus Christ. There is only one reason why Jesus is the Great Physician and that is because He is our Divine Saviour. Salvation is more than a cure for hysteria. It is a crucifixion followed by resurrection. Problem preaching can become a real pampering of a person's pesky self. When one by faith in Jesus Christ puts off the old man by putting him down and out, the act of putting off the old man becomes a process of putting on the new man in Christ. When the old man is put off and down and out, the complexes, jitters, hysterias, hallucinations and lunacies go with it. Thematic Christian preaching, including thematic topical preaching, is not tinkering, not putting salve on symptoms, not idolizing sick minds and making menial curtsies. It is opening flood gates of Divine purgation and blowing up dams so that the sea of God's grace can sweep over the continent of human personality. What is the use of getting overflowing crowds into the sanctuary and being called great and wonderful if all you do is to administer mental nose-drops and moral throat-spray? What is the ultimate value if you tickle their ears with dramatic or humorous stories and they alternately weep and laugh and go off to say, "Isn't he wonderful?" A "great" preacher who achieves what the world calls phenomenal success has a lot to answer for. You cannot hee-haw people into the Kingdom of God. The world, yea the Church, crucified Jesus and when they almost deify one of his preachers, it may be this preacher's church which is meant in Rev. 3:20 where Christ is on the outside knocking on locked doors to get in.

A second weakness of topical preaching is the difficulty of observing the principle of unity. Even if the topical preacher guards against forsaking the Bible and against rambling the wide world over, the terrain of Scripture is so vast and any great Biblical topic so Scripturally spacious that the topical preacher is apt to bite off much more than either he or his people can chew or swallow. Take Matt. 10:32, "Every one therefore who shall confess me before men, him also will I confess before my Father who is in heaven." You decide to take from this verse the idea of confessing Christ. You intend to preach on the topic, "Confessing Christ." You start out by seeing what you can do with the topic before you undertake special study. You make some useful notes but you are not satisfied. Your efforts at theme construction prove unsatisfactory.

You turn now to the treatment of the subject in a Bible dictionary, a dictionary of Christ and the Gospels, and in commentaries on the various Scriptures presented. The result of this is a number of points. Confessing Christ: I. What it means. II. Why important? III. Why difficult? IV. Why necessary? V. What It Costs. VI. What it does for you. VII. What it means to others. VIII. What it gets you in the end. IX. What it means to God.

Theme construction has results like this: Confessing Christ is: 1, a testimony to life's most wonderful experience; 2, a revelation of life's deepest convictions; 3, the test of the reality of personal devotion and loyalty to the Saviour; 4, God's technique for the spread of the Gospel; 5, the price and guarantee of imperishable glory; 6, a person's only chance of qualifying for acceptance with God; 7, the secret of giving life its highest possible significance; 8, the key to the most dynamic and far-reaching personal influence.

Past instruction in the science and art of preaching has always emphasized that in thematic preaching the divisions of a sermon must be clearly expressed or implied in the theme. If you cannot get satisfactory divisions, it means that your theme is inadequate. As sure as you get the right theme your divisions will come like doves to their window. You may conclude that the right theme is too long and cannot be readily memorized by the people. How can you make it simpler and still retain divisions either stated or implied? This calls for work, so exhaustingly costly, but yielding as benefits, power to think, power to express, ever larger background, power to concentrate, fresh insights, clarity of aim, growing competence, enrichment of life and influence and other surplus values.

When you try to construct a theme with all the divisions in it or as many divisions as you want, you soon begin to appraise the points already tentatively accepted. Perhaps they can be boiled down to three or four divisions with promise of unity in the sermon. To preach on the topic, "Confessing Christ" certainly calls for an explanation of what it means to confess Christ. That is properly a first division. Secondly, it ought to be pointed out what it costs to confess Christ. There you have Division two. Thirdly, as an inducement, it is well to explain the benefits or rewards of confessing Christ. We now have Division three. You still do not have a theme. It seems to square with the way things go in sermon preparation to get points or divisions first and theme last of all. You take notes during your preparatory study. By the time you start to write a theme, you have several points which seem to have the stature of divisions. Then you begin to reason and to ask questions. What does it mean to confess Christ? What does it cost? What good does it do? There you have three divisions and as yet no theme. Look at them: I. The meaning of confessing Christ. II. The cost of confessing Christ. III. The results of confessing Christ. Your temptation now will be to preach these three points without getting a theme embracing them. It may seem very easy for a congregation to remember three such clear points or questions. But suppose, now, that you can get a simple, positive, constructive, short, Christian sentence for the theme of your sermon, something timeless and therefore always contemporaneous, a sentence easy to remember, of which your divisions will be aspects!

Before proceeding with the matter of the theme, however, you want to go over all your points again to see if several you are omitting are more important than the three you have tentatively selected. It becomes evident that all the points and questions you had can be fittingly and pertinently answered in the three divisions selected. In the third division, for example, on the results of confessing Christ it will appear very clearly how important and necessary confession of Christ is. When discussing the cost of confessing Christ in the second division, you will naturally have occasion to portray the cost in terms of the difficulties. So Division I on the meaning of confessing Christ will in measure cover other points not specifically announced as divisions.

If all the nine questions raised had been retained as divisions, a theme containing or implying them all would have been almost impossible. You might have made some attempts as follows:

1. Confessing Christ has such importance and confers such benefits, that whatever the cost, it is a Christian's most urgent and imperative challenge. 22 words.

2. Nothing is more significant or important or rewarding, however costly, than confessing personal faith in Jesus Christ as Saviour and Lord. 21 words.

3. Confessing Christ means so much and has such far-reaching consequences that whatever the cost, it has to be done. 20 words.

Such long themes are ruled out because they do not measure up to specifications and are too hard to remember. What is wanted is a brief statement, joyous if possible, that people will want to remember, that is a thrust from God, as it were, right straight through their hearts. With only three divisions embracing three times that many points or ideas we wrote this for a theme: Confessing Christ is the costly road to the grandest results. The three divisions are in it and we expected to let it go at that. But a thematic Christian preacher can always look at it again and make another try. You never can tell in what moment a flash beyond the brightness of the sun at noon comes straight from God to fill you with holy laughter. But what, pray, is the objection to the ten word theme suggested? The words "the costly road" stand right in the middle of that theme and make it look like a camel or a hunch-back. The costly road has to be in the theme because the price of confessing Christ has to be paid. But you do not have to protrude that costly road and make it stick out like a sore finger. The martyrs sang while being burned at the stake and rejoiced that they were counted worthy to suffer for Christ's sake. "That costly road" therefore has to be paved with gold and made a shining "King's Highway." The thing that has to be prominent is the immeasurable, glorious and eternal results, benefits, rewards, achievements by God's grace of confessing Christ. No sooner seen than said, for God gives words as well as thoughts. You are going to preach a thematic topical sermon on "Confessing Christ." Text Matt. 10:32. Theme, "Confessing Christ is worth all it costs." Halleluiah! Only seven words! The word "worth" is now the center and summit of your theme. That is the word you want there. What God will do for you now in this present world and throughout eternity by means of and because of your confessing Christ and what He will do for others on the same scale for the same reason is all in that word "worth." Your divisions are all in your theme: the meaning, the cost and the results of confessing Christ. The results are going to dominate the atmosphere of your sermon. Already you are singing, "O, could I speak the matchless word, O could I sound the glories forth, Which in my Saviour shine!" Your closing hymn, too, is already music in your soul, as well as the middle hymn just cited. In the opening hymn you worship God. In the middle hymn you sing about Jesus. In the closing hymn you try to get people to do something about it. "Ashamed of Jesus, sooner far, Let evening blush to own a star."

In such manner is a thematic topical sermon constructed. It must be Biblical. Please use a text. As your soul liveth, pray and work for a dynamic theme, a short one with a punch. Encourage your people to keep a diary on your preaching, to write down your texts, topics, themes, divisions and other impressive thoughts and impressions. If you know that they do it, you will be strengthened with might in the inner man to climb the steep ascent of thematic preaching power and all your members will have documentary proof of your faithfulness unto death to the souls entrusted to your pastoral care.

It is wonderful how the divisions of even a thematic topical sermon can be aspects of a simple, vital theme. The different aspects of a theme which we call divisions seem to coalesce, to merge, to represent one action or a totality of result seen from different angles. Take John 8:12, "I am the light of the world: he that followeth me shall not walk in darkness, but shall have the light of life." You choose to preach a topical sermon on "Christ, the light of the world." You take that part of the teaching of your text and go your sermonic way. You decide to study the subject of light and to use the ideas you gain about light as a frame in which to hang your portrait of Jesus as the light of the world. You learn that if there were no sun or moon or stars to shine and no other source of light, everything would be just total darkness. Light transforms darkness into its own self. You take in the transforming power of light. When the light of whatever kind is turned on, you can see what's what and you take in the revealing power of light. A picture of a lighthouse or a radio program puts you in mind of the guiding power of light. You recall also the cheering power of light and already you have four points to illustrate a possible theme that Christ is this dark world's light. You decide from a sense of theological propriety to take the second idea first and there you are. Sermon subject: How Significant Is Jesus: Text, John 8:12. Theme, "Christ is this dark world's light." Divisions: I. Christ is a revealing light. II. Christ is a transforming light. III. Christ is a guiding light. IV. Christ is a cheering light. Now the point is, this light, which is Christ, is one light and when He is let in, He exercises this fourfold power of light all at once. He is the answer to all questions and problems. When eyes are opened by Him, the heart is transformed, one's nature changed. In the same process, you find out where you are to go. Christ is your guiding light. He sets the joybells ringing in the heart. Christ is a cheering light. What a light! What a Christ! "The people that sat in darkness" saw a great light when they saw Christ. He shines in the heart to give "the light of the knowledge of the glory of God." He reveals, transforms, guides and cheers, all at once, unifying everything into one broad stream of radiant living. Truly, "the light of the world is Jesus." It takes a thematic Christian preacher to hold up Christ the light of all our seeing and the world's true light.

# XI

# Thematic Topical Preaching — Special Form

THEMATIC Christian preaching offers plenty of variety in sermon styles. An extension of the idea of topical sermons may now be considered. It is a topical sermon with a verse of Scripture introducing each division, the verse thus used containing the teaching to be developed. Since in thematic preaching the divisions are aspects and developments of the theme, the significance of using a verse of Scripture at the beginning of each division is that a verse of Scripture either serves as the logical statement of the division or precedes it, being given between the rhetorical statement of the division and the logical statement of it. It is a form of thematic preaching which guarantees the Biblical character of a sermon.

To illustrate, take Nebuchadnezzar's "Dream of the Tree" as recorded in the book of Daniel, chapter four. It is the astonishing story of a wicked heathen king. The story is told as the king himself told it. You are surprised at the outset when the king says, "It hath seemed good unto me to show the signs and the wonders that the Most High God hath wrought towards me." What a remark to come from such a man! You are in search of a sermon. It warms your heart that Nebuchadnezzar the king should have learned his own place so well as to speak of God as "the Most High God." A sensitive heart at once sees giant scales in one of which all the kings of the earth are put. Down goes the scale with all these men of weight. A reverent imagination now pictures God in the other scale and down it comes. The kings are seen as a speck of dust in the balance with no weight at all in comparison with the Most High God. The expression. "The Most High God" is already, not only in your mental incubator, but deep in your spiritual sensorium, as a possible sermon subject.

Three times in the chapter the Divine purpose of Nebuchadnezzar's tragic experience is expressed, "that the living may know that the Most High ruleth in the kingdom of men." Decision is made to preach a topical sermon on these words as a text. Memory recalls a woman who in wartime fairly shouted, "What is the matter with God? Why does He not do something?" Others, less frenzied, nevertheless have argued that if God is love and almighty, He should and would show His hand. A sermon seems always in order on "The Divine Administration" or "God's Government Of The World." Text and topic are thus taken care of.

What happened to Nebuchadnezzar is seen to have been a penalty for wicked behaviour and a redemptive technique on God's part to bring the great but bad man to a better life. It was not in vain that he was punished and suffered, because he gives his experience a great ending, "Now I, Nebuchadnezzar, praise and extol and honor the King of heaven, for all his works are truth, and his ways justice; and those that walk in pride he is able to abase." He became able to say with the Psalmist, "It was good for me that I was afflicted." His great statement has timeless pertinence to man's impertinence before God.

Quest for a theme finally yields this: "God's government of mankind sets the standard for human behaviour." Meanwhile, a Christmas hymn is singing in your soul, "Joy to the world, the Lord is come." You cast anchor at the stanza which starts, "He rules the world with truth and grace." A noun is better than a pronoun. The hymn sings about Jesus. The coming of God to man is fulfilled in Him. Jesus is Immanuel, God with us. "Christ rules the world with truth and grace." The words "God" and "Christ" can here be used synonymously and interchangeably. Since the text is from the Old Testament, the theme-song of your sermon may well be, "God rules the world with truth and grace." The children also will remember it. A familiar hymn will ever after have memorable association as soon as the sermon is preached.

When you really get going on sermon construction, things break so fast that you hardly know what to seize and put down first. Divisions are staring you in the face and begging with open arms for a reservation in the driver's seat, but another hymn stands hard by, is even already a melody in the heart. What connection can there possibly be between the hymn "The sands of time are sinking" and a sermon on "God's Government of Mankind?" Just listen, "With mercy and with judgment, My web of time He wove; And e'en the dews of sorrow, were lustered by His love." That comes close home to many people and guarantees a tender passage somewhere in the sermon when heart speaks to heart.

Now for divisions. Topic: God's Government of the World. Text: Daniel 4, 17: "The Most High ruleth in the kingdom of men." Theme: God rules the world with truth and grace. Divisions: I. The Fact of God's Rule. Instead now of following the rhetorical statement of this division with the usual logical statement such as, "God rules the World," you introduce one or more Scriptural verses which state the fact of God's rule over mankind. One strong verse expressive of God's universal and everlasting dominion will suffice, although parallel verses of similar significance may be quoted as the development of the division proceeds. The idea is that the verse now quoted is expressive of the aspect of text and theme to be developed in the division.

How is a preacher to find the right verse to introduce each division? This suggests the importance of a competent Bible Concordance and the wisdom of using it constantly. Need it be said what words to look up in the concordance in order to establish Scripturally the reign of God? No minister has "the lay of the land" in sermon preparation and construction unless he browses periodically both in the concordance and in various kinds of Bible and religious encyclopaedias. On the text suggested it would be a feast to read the Psalms, recording all the verses which bear on the three divisions of the theme. What a wealth of verses there would be, illustrative of each divisional aspect of the theme! To avoid indiscriminate use of these verses calls for a careful consideration of the idea of purpose disclosed in the verse out of which the text was taken. God acts as He does because He wants men to know that the Most High rules in the kingdom of men. The verses quoted at the head of divisions will have the same atmosphere of Divine intention and the whole sermon will thus be a unity.

Take, now, the division: The Fact of God's rule. Psalm 9, verse 7, says, "But Jehovah sitteth as king forever," and Psalm 7, verse 8, "Jehovah ministereth judgment to the peoples." The first expresses the idea of God as eternal King, that is, that the everlasting God exercises rule over mankind. God is always on the job as the ruler of men. The second emphasizes God's moral government of men. When God is said to minister judgment to peoples, the meaning is not fully covered when it is said that God penalizes wrong-doing. The meaning rather is that God administers justice, that is to say, governs mankind on moral principles. It is apparent that this second quotation may possibly be of service in a later division. Looking at the theme, "God rules the world with truth and grace" suggests three divisions: I. God rules the world. II. God rules the world with truth. III. God rules the world with grace. These are logical statements of the divisions. They may be stated rhetorically as follows: I. The Fact of God's rule of mankind. II. The character of God's rule of mankind. III. The Purpose of God's rule of mankind. The rhetorical statement of divisions is always first, followed normally by the logical statement.

The new type of thematic topical sermon calls for a Scripture verse or verses between the rhetorical and logical statements of divisions. If two or more verses are quoted, they must be identical in meaning and sound a united witness on the aspect of the theme to be developed in the division. The reason for this caution and counsel is that a topical sermon of this kind is apt to become as many sermons in one as there are divisions. One reason this type of topical preaching is frowned upon by teachers of preaching is because of the tendency to give three or four sermons when the order of the day calls for one. It will be seen that sticking to the theme is of basic importance. No matter what fine Scriptures or thoughts have to be ruled out as irrelevant, it should be a categorical imperative to stick to the theme and to put everything irrelevant to it in a humanitarian concentration camp.

Division II, on The Character of God's Rule, might use Psalm 99, verse 1, "Jehovah reigns; let the people tremble." Verses stressing the righteousness and justice of God can readily be found. The verse chosen is in harmony with the purpose of God's dealing with Nebuchadnezzar, to impress a heathen monarch with his moral obligations. The verse almost shouts the righteousness and justice of God, indicating the proper response of people when they learn that "all's Law." It is intended to warn people of the moral order of the universe, of the folly of defying God and of the certainty that no one can put anything over on God. This is directly in line with the text, with the theme and with Division II : God rules the world with truth.  One recalls Emerson's essay on Compensation and the law of poetic justice in the Greek tragedians and the immortal works of fiction, to say nothing of the plays of Shakespeare. What scope there is in this sermon to speak to humanity which, with the arrogance of unbelief, is always trying to put something over on God. Man must learn that he is face to face with the moral structure of the universe and with the holy indignation of a righteous Judge.

Division III on "The Purpose of God's Rule of Mankind," might use Psalm 97, verse 1, between the rhetorical statement and the logical, "Jehovah reigneth, let the earth rejoice." How natural to say after this verse, "God rules the world with grace." Though God deals with man in righteousness, God's punitive in this world is redemptive. Many wonderful Scriptures can readily be found to show that God's laws and commandments are highways of true self-realization and self-expresssion, techniques for making human life a vast moral splendor and ways leading to fulness of achievement, service and enjoyment. Psalm 19 can be our teacher concerning God's ordinances that "in keeping them there is great reward."

A sermon like this on God's moral government of the world, with Scripture introducing the whole and each separate division, becomes a unified message moving with balanced progress to a wonderful climax on "the grace of God that bringeth salvation." The greatest problems of life here come to the clarity of lucid simplicity. The mystery of iniquity has its explanation in man's moral freedom and in his evil heart of unbelief. The mystery of suffering has its explanation in God's redeeming purpose. "With mercy and with judgment" is the title of God's dealings with us. Perhaps it might be well to give summary statement of what is now clear in outline.

Sermon subject: God's Government of the World.   Text: Daniel 4, either verse 17, 25, or 32, "The Most High ruleth in the kingdom of men. Theme: God rules the world with truth and grace. Division I. The Fact of God's Rule. "But Jehovah sitteth as King forever." (Psalm 9:7) God rules the world. Division II. The Character of God's Rule. "Jehovah reigneth, let the people tremble." (Psalm 99:1) God rules the world with truth. Division III. The Purpose of God's Rule. "Jehovah reigneth; let the earth rejoice." (Psalm 97:1) God rules the world with grace. It is a great day for a Christian when he learns that God has no pampered and spoiled children. God deals with men, to be sure, from the standpoint of their behaviour, but also from the standpoint of their possibilities. With sermons like the one suggested, a preacher can help people to a true, that is to say, to the Christian philosophy of life. He can school them in the moral structure of the universe, in the righteousness and grace of God and in the purgative, constructive aspects of the rough side of life.

Does anyone see any structural fault in the above outline? If so, make necessary corrections. There seems to be unity, progress, balance, symmetry and climax. It is the outline of a new type of thematic topical sermon, using one Bible verse or passage for the text and additional Bible verses for the divisions, the verses for the divisions being like their rhetorical and logical statements, aspects of the theme, thus guaranteeing unity, progress and climax of thematic development and schooling the preacher to make more and more use of the Bible in his sermons.

It has often occurred to the author that if two or more ministers could club together and agree on a course of sermons, they might have regular get-to-gethers to share the products of their toil. The result would be the elimination of competition between churches in the same community, the general elevation of pulpit ministry, inducement to all clergy thus federated to study harder so as to bring a larger contribution to the regular preaching conferences and sorely needed help to less gifted preachers or ministers sermonically temporarily below par for good reason. Thus would be set up a system or regime of sermonic socialism under which God's servants would have all things in common, the "all things" referring to the doctrines of grace. The brilliant man would have conspicuous compensation for sharing light by inward foretastes of the Master's final, "Well done" and a possible lazy one would be inspired or shamed into digging his one talent out of the ground. In an age when churches get tired of their preachers and preachers get tired of their churches, it may be laid down as canonically axiomatic that preachers ought to mean more to one another. A weekly session or two for sermonic thought exchange with possible fellowship of intercession might prove a lever to lift many a bankrupt clergyman into exhilarating solvency. Denominational animosities or interdenominational feuds would find the going hard where ministers are kindly affectioned enough toward one another to share sermon material for next Sunday. Persistent lack of cooperation would likewise gasp and die. This business of saying, "I am of Paul, I am of Apollos, I am of Cephas" deserves the death-blow which only sermonic socialism among preachers can give it.

Thematic topical preaching is never to be underestimated. It is a possible technique for genuine Biblical preaching. Where preparation is conscientious and thorough, the study of a single topic may lead to several possible outlines or ways of treating the subject. In the outline suggested, an earlier theme was brushed aside. Look at it again: "God's government of mankind sets the standard for human behaviour." Division I. The Character of God's government. 1. A government of law. 2. A government of love. II. The Extent of God's Government. 1. All men. 2. All circumstances. III. The Purpose of God's government. 1. Individual redemption. 2. Social transformation. A preacher can go to town with an outline like that.

In Division II of the first outline, mention was made of the certainty that "no one can put anything over on God." A sermon could be preached on the theme, "No one can ever put anything over on God." The text can be the same as in the other two outlines. "The Most High ruleth in the kingdom of men." Division I. The Universal Attempt To Put Something Over on God. II. The Failure Of All Attempts To Put Something Over On God. III. The Reason For the Failure to Put Something Over On God. God's character: His righteousness and love. The moral order of the universe. The futility of trying to circumvent an all-holy, all-loving, almighty, all-wise God. Questions in line with the above suggest themselves. Why and how do people try to put over something on God? How do they succeed? Why do they fail? Instead, now, of having one outline for a thematic topical sermon, there are three, still to be worked at, no doubt, but real enough and pointed to indicate that if preachers will pay the price of toil and prayer necessary to thematic sermon construction they will in due time reap rich crops by developing an art which will never fail them, because God blesses the faithfulness of His servants and by certifying to their people that they are work-men who need not be ashamed. It is thrilling to contemplate how dynamic and significant thematic topical preaching can be when it sticks to Scripture and makes the theme determinative of what goes into a sermon. Unless a preacher unceasingly prays "Break Thou the Bread of life to me, to me," how is he going to feed His congregation with bread from heaven? But it can be done and it must be done to bring the Christian pulpit to prophetic, apostolic, Pentecostal and redemptive stature.

Having spent time in Daniel four, it is seen that Nebuchad-nezzar was a bad man. He was warned. He disregarded the warning. He got what was coming to him. He learned his lesson. Can this be another sermon waiting to be born? Things like this are being said by the inner voice: No one is finally lost without being warned and spurning God's offered grace. God gives a man what he has coming to him, but always in order to save him from a far worse fate. Here are promising thoughts. Let who will, dwell on them. You can be a good preacher, but you had better school yourself to be a thematic one. Take any great sermon published and assimilate it suf-ficiently to transform it into a thematic one, and the result will be an absolutely and astonishingly original production. Thematic Christian preaching is the end of all plagiarism. Read all the sermons you want to read. If you take one and change it to a thematic sermon, by the time you are done, it will be yours like a laborer's pay after a hard week of toil. You have to incarnate a truth before you can make it livingly thematic. If you produce a thematic sermon which is a living organism, God brought it to birth through you. It's yours. It's yours from God. It is no longer Chrysostom's or Calvin's or Luther's or Barth's. Plagiarism is a mosquito sucking the blood out of arm or leg. But only a mosquito can live on such a small quantity. Thematic sermon construction is the production and donation of blood plasma to save dying souls from spiritual starvation and to nourish the members of God's redeemed family. The uni-verse is a brotherly, cooperative affair. Life ministers to life; blood to blood. The scarlet thread of sacrifice which runs through Scripture runs through the universe and everything in it. The artist, who painted more beautifully than others but who died in bringing his conception to perfect artistic ex-pression, had mixed his blood with his paints. He went down to get up and literally died to live. So the thematic Christian preacher bleeds to bless, always ready to be offered, pouring life out and paying it down to be God's spokesman of resur-rection in a world dead in trespasses and sin.

# XII

## Thematic Textual Preaching

A THEMATIC textual sermon is one that draws topic, theme and divisions out of a single text of Scripture. A sermon on a single verse of Scripture, explaining the truth of that verse, doing it completely to the extent of making the development of the sermon the unfolding of the text, is a textual sermon. A thematic textual sermon is a sermon constructed on a plan drawn from the text. The name of a thematic textual sermon, the thematic truth, the sermon body in outline, all come from the teaching of the text.

It is usually quite possible to expound the meaning of a single verse of Scripture in one sermon, especially if it is done thematically and sermonically. It is always to be remembered that thematic and sermonic are the important words. Real preaching is ideally sermonic in form and the ideal sermonic form is thematic. It cannot be too persistently impressed that the sermon is a unique form for the oral presentation of Gospel truth and that the ideal sermon form is always the thematic.

The thematic textual sermon differs from the thematic topical sermon in that it sticks to the one text and does not venture abroad in search of divisions. It does not extract or deduce a topic from a text in order to explore the topic in its own suggestiveness or in its wider Biblical significance. It takes a selected text as the measure and the blue-print of truth to be presented, looks to it for what is to be presented and developed and keeps looking to it for the lines of development called divisions. A professor of Church History once said that when he had read a sermon of F. W. Robertson of Brighton, he felt there was nothing more to be said about the text. Robertson said it all and the professor was hard put to it to preach on it with originality. Robertson was a most able textual preacher, but excellent as his sermons are from the standpoint of faithfulness to the text and adequacy of divisions, he came short in adherence to thematic structure and so in thematic unity. Thematic textual preaching is a magnificent technique for giving a text of Scripture the floor and letting it say all there is in it to say.

Thematic textual preaching differs from thematic expository preaching in its exhaustive treatment of a text, whereas in thematic expository preaching, the preacher has to select from several possible topics and themes, choosing one which is to be as exhaustively treated in thematic sermon form as the Scripture passage together with parallel passages allows. The expository preacher draws topic, theme, divisions and divisional material from the passage of Scripture to be expounded, but the thematic sermonic form enables him to treat in his sermon either a primary or a subordinate truth and to omit what lies outside his thematic outline.

A thematic textual sermon is limited to one verse of Scripture but the verse has to be big enough to furnish divisions as well as topic and theme. A preacher might get an idea for a sermon out of a full verse of Scripture or out of a part of one. If neither a full verse or a part of one furnishes the lines of thematic development called divisions, the resulting sermon is not textual but topical. No sermon can be textual which is not based on a verse of Scripture. A preacher who preaches without taking a text from Scripture may be a Biblical preacher in the sense of reflecting Biblical thought, but he cannot be a textual preacher. A textual sermon is a sermon based on a text from Scripture, the text being a complete verse and the complete verse being comprehensive enough to furnish the topic, the theme and the lines of development of the theme known as divisions.

A sermon is called textual because its thematic outline, including divisions, sticks to the text, does not fall short of it by having less divisions than the verse calls for nor goes beyond it by adding one or more divisions not found in the verse. What has been said does not mean that a textual preacher is debarred from explaining the Scriptural setting of his text or from quoting other Bible verses. The point is that in textual preaching the text is commander-in-chief, the text being a single verse of Scripture with enough content to qualify for the office; and the preacher's theme-song in making his thematic outline is, "Where it leads me, I will follow." The verse which is text has to be explained, the thematic sermonic form is the way to do it and the textual preacher is the man. The sermon body of a textual sermon is a development along lines laid down in the verse which serves as text.

It must be admitted that the Christian preaching of American pulpits does not observe these discriminations as between topical, textual and expository types of sermon. A topical preacher may before the sermon is over become textual enough to give the full explanation of a text or expository enough to give either the primary or subordinate meaning of a passage of Scripture. A textual preacher may suffer divisional prostration and parachute into tropical and topical green pastures. An expository preacher with passage of Scripture for wide domain may for a time have great liberty in one of the many verses under consideration and give F. W. Robertson a close run on textual preeminence. There is no law of the Medes and Persians in the matter which changes not. Types of preaching and sermon styles are intended as directives and techniques for organizing and presenting sermonic thought and Scripture teaching. They are aids to definiteness, intended to qualify a preacher for turning a pulpit into a throne. There is a way to develop the muscles, learn how to write or speak or sing, and master the art of thinking and meditation. Why should there not be aids to preaching: forms, techniques, types and styles of sermon preparation, construction and delivery, calculated to improve its reception by the people, its compatibility with Scripture and its general elevation as an accepted way of doing a masterly job? It is pertinent for a preacher to keep refreshing his ideals and purposes with questions like this: "How do we start? Where do we go? What can be done to meet the plight of man?"

A thematic textual preacher makes up his mind to get the full meaning of a verse into his system and then to share it with his people in hope that they may get it into their systems, too. Here is Hebrews 2:3, "How shall we escape if we neglect so great salvation?" This is not the whole of the verse. The rest of verse three, as well as verses two and four, ought to be taken with it and the full passage would then call for an expository sermon. If you take the whole of verse three, you can preach a textual sermon on it, "How shall we escape if we neglect so great salvation? which having at the first been spoken through the Lord, was confirmed unto us by them that heard." Usually the question alone is used for a text and made the basis of an evangelistic sermon. If you take the whole verse, you get the impression that the question it contains is addressed to Christians, to those who have salvation, that is, to the Church. The whole verse tells how the great salvation came to the Hebrew Christians to whom the epistle is addressed. Questions like the following are proper. 1. What is salvation? 2. In what sense is salvation great? 3. How do those who have it neglect it? 4. What is the result of this neglect? Rhetorically stated the divisions would be: I. The meaning of salvation. II. The greatness of salvation. III. The neglect of salvation. IV. The penalty of neglecting salvation. A first try at a theme might yield this: Salvation possessed but neglected means inescapable penalty. Try your own hand at it. These questions and divisions are all in the question of the text, but no question or division has been suggested for the rest of the verse. One could put the meaning of the rest of the verse into the introduction. You could start out by saying something like this: "Our text contains a question addressed to the early Christians of the apostolic church. The knowledge of Christ and His salvation had come to them first through Jesus Himself and then through His redeemed servants. They had responded to it, received the great salvation which Christ died to bestow, but already thus early in Christian history, those who had salvation were disposed to disregard its ethical and social significance. They themselves, to whom the Epistle to the Hebrews was addressed, were saved through the passion for souls of others, but they could rejoice in it and go about their usual business, forgetting that the business of propagating the Christian faith is fundamental to retaining it and to bringing in the better world made possible by the redemption which is in Christ."

The text, rightly considered, calls for a trenchant message to a church which does not act up to the significance of the salvation which it claims to possess. It is a message against the religious indifference of professing Christians. A Christian without a testimony cannot escape inevitable consequences. A Christian has to pay the penalty of just doing nothing for Christ. Already more striking themes are stirring within. Get your own heart warmed up. Our business is a thematic textual sermon on Heb. 2:3. We have shown how the whole verse can be utilized in presenting a powerful message from God to an indifferent or worldly church. A certain wealthy woman put most of her wealth into jewels and kept them in lock-boxes in the bank. She got no income from them. She was afraid to have them in the house for fear they might be stolen. She kept her wealth in jewels under lock and key in a bank. You cannot do that with salvation. "Trade ye herewith" is the Divine imperative. The verse, Hebrews 2:3, is a tremendous challenge to the Church. The Church, as an institution, is always in process of creation and recreation as an organization of redeemed people, first by the members keeping their salvation up-to-date in the interest of fresh witness and secondly, by acceptance of Christ on the part of others through the preaching and the testimony. A textual thematic sermon on Hebrews 2:3 is sure to put everybody straight on the meaning of the verse and on a very vital matter. It is something immense to keep a church alive. The menace of apostasy, worldliness, and powerlessness is always an active threat. It must be evident what a vast service thematic textual preaching can render. It is a curtailment of a preacher's personal liberty in order that the real meaning of a verse may get under his skin and the restrictions he has placed upon himself may issue in the liberty of the Spirit of God.

It will be understood that Hebrews 2:3, addressed as it is to the Church, is thus also a message from God to individual Christians. It is the individual Christian's personal response to the challenge of the text through which the response of the Church as a whole is registered. The thematic textual sermon on Hebrews 2:3, will therefore be made as pointed as possible to the individual Christian. Look again at the suggested theme, "Salvation possessed but neglected means inescapable penalty." There are two possible objections to the theme thus expressed. The word "possessed" might arouse a spirit of argument and controversy. It might quicken speculative interest in the question whether a person who is once a Christian is always a Christian. Your aim in this sermon on Hebrews 2:3 is practical and presented to get the people to do something actual about being a Christian. The second possible objection is the use of the words "salvation," "inescapable" and "penalty." These words are all useful, legitimate and expressive but are they as easily understood by the people in the pews as they might be? The word "salvation" is the very heart of the Christian message, but what does it say without due explanation to the hearers? A theme must be as simple, as impressive and challenging as possible. The theme has only eight words but to boys and girls they might seem big, stilted, stock, words, not speaking the language of the world as teen age uses it.

The more one thinks on the text, pondering its real essence, the clearer it becomes that the verse with its challenging question constitutes an appeal, a challenge, an urge and reveals a solemn necessity to do something about this matter of having so great salvation, this matter of being a Christian. It becomes ever more evident that most weighty considerations demand that a Christian show his colors. What say? O for a tongue, the theme has come! Here it is: "A Christian must show his colors or face the consequences." Nothing staid or stilted or stock about that! A high-school lad might like it like this,

"A Christian must show his colors or else." Have it your own way but the professor sticks to the ten word theme. Imagine ringing the changes on such a theme in a textual sermon. The heart of the text is in it. That is what the text means to say and urge. The words "show your colors" are right there in the place of prominence in the theme. The thrust of the theme is in those three words. The thrust of the text is there also.

The question now is, How to preach the text with such a theme. You might start with a few questions. 1. What it means to show your colors as a Christian. 2. Why should a Christian show his colors? 3. How does a Christian fail to show his colors? 4. What happens if Christians do not show their colors? When it was said, "Start with a few questions," the reference of course is to sermon preparation, not to public presentation. Only the finished product appears in the pulpit. Questions 1 and 3 seem to be identical. Start, therefore, with question 2 and make it the first. Here is the set-up. I. Reasons for showing your colors as a Christian. II. Failures to show your colors as a Christian. III. Consequences of not showing your colors as a Christian. On Division I, the text presents three reasons: 1. you have salvation, you are a saved man, you are a Christian. Under this subdivision you explain the word salvation, discussing it perhaps as a past experience and a present process to culminate in a glorious future consummation. The second reason is subdivision 2 and is this, The salvation you have is so great that it challenges expression in ethical living and testimony. You ask, In what sense is salvation so great? You answer and say things like this. (a) It is great as a Divine technique or concept. Who but God could ever have thought of such a way of saving rebel man? (b.) It is great in the love which inspired it and which it expresses. (c.) It is great in being a Gospel for an entire lost world. Christ is "the propitiation not for our sins only but for the sins of the whole world." (d.) It is a salvation commensurate with the needs of the total human life of total human personality. The third reason is subdivision 3 of Division I. The

Christian faith has to be propagated. Here you can state the significance of that part of the text which follows the question it contains. Salvation is spread by the testimony of witnesses. If you use this part of the text in this subdivision, you need not put it in the introduction. This makes the body of the sermon more perfectly textual and gives liberty to start with a more striking introduction if God crowns preparation with holy fire.

Division II treats of failures to show your colors as a Christian. It might seem a shorter Division than the first one. It all depends on the preacher. The idea of Division II is certainly in the text in the word "neglect." This division discusses how Christians neglect their salvation; that is to say, how they fail to show their colors as Christians. The general answer to the question is, "By doing nothing." There are a thousand ways in which the individual Christian does nothing. Here are some: neglect of the means of grace, lack of missionary interest and zeal, turning deaf ears to appeals for cooperation and service. There are many ways in which the local church and the Church at large does nothing. Church History can witness here, as also the state of the Church in the modern world. Multitudes sweep past the Church in great cities, milling through famous streets past famous churches. Hundreds of thousands who bear the name of Christian thus pass by with no urge to go in. Well might a modern prophet cry, "Is it nothing to you who pass by?" or "Turn ye, O turn ye, for why will you die?" Christian indifference is such an immense area not only "the wide world over" but throughout past ages, that there is no reason why Division II should be shorter than Division I and disturb the balance of the sermon.

Division III treats consequences. These are not given in the text, but the idea of inescapable consequences of not showing your colors for Christ is definitely taught by direct implication. A preacher can get going by asking questions in his own mind. What happens to a Christian personally when he does nothing to make it evident that he is a Christian? He loses the joy of salvation. He cripples his influence. If he is a family man he does his family a gross injustice. He fails to take up the whole armour of God and meets mortal enemies of his soul unprepared. He handicaps his Christian life and mortgages his soul. What happens to a local church when it has no evangelistic and missionary zeal? What happens to the Church as a whole when secularism and hierarchical despotism are in the seats of the mighty? It is clear what a strong climax can be given to the third division of the sermon body when once the preacher sees and feels what both individual Christians and local churches miss through failure of real consecration. To know what might be and to realize what actually is impresses the tragedy of not showing your colors as Christians. Here it will be appropriate to describe to what extent the Christian Church is responsible for world conditions.

A thematic textual sermon on Hebrews 2:3 may very well conclude with an appeal to Christians to reconsecrate themselves to their Saviour and Lord and to the unsaved to give their hearts to Christ. If Christians are given priority in the exposition of the text, it is evident that dire consequences attend failure to accept Jesus as personal Saviour. The thematic textual preacher wields a mighty weapon for Christ and His kingdom by taking a verse of Scripture and getting from it a full plan for a sermon which will implement the text and be a channel of its Divine significance and power. Sticking to textual topic, textual theme and textual divisions, the preacher can freight these with the full significance of a specific part of God's self-revelation, using the sermonic form with its thematic pointedness to drive God's truth home.

# XIII

## Thematic Doctrinal Preaching

DOCTRINAL preaching is by its very nature the most basic form of preaching because it is always on a Bible verse or passage which contains truth rather than counsel or exhortation. The entire Bible is a vast continent of truth, but there are areas which constitute the redemptive facts of Bible religion and there are areas which cover personal and social ethical implications. Doctrinal preaching is proclamation of the foundations of Christian faith. Broad streams of revelation run through Scripture, showing the truth pertaining to salvation. Countless tributaries flow from, not into, these mighty streams, tributaries of practical implications, revealing duty. Doctrinal preaching is the big steamer that does business on the main streams. Sermons which base their message on Bible disclosures of duty are cargo ships which dot the tributaries.

A thematic doctrinal sermon is one based on a Bible verse or passage or sentence which sets forth a redemptive truth of God's self-revelation. A single verse may on occasion be like a longer passage in having several doctrines within itself. Here thematic procedure is a life-saver. Thematic sermon construction requires a preacher to select one doctrine for special emphasis. The doctrine selected is put in the theme and given the place of honor there, so that it is indicated that the doctrine thus stressed is to have major exposition. The other doctrines in the verse or passage need not be ignored but their presentation is subordinate, showing their relation to the doctrine which is given thematic and sermonic priority. All the doctrines in selected Bible texts have some degree of mutual relation or fellowship but as sure as a sentence has a subject, so surely some one specific doctrine is seen to have preeminence in a particular spot in Scripture and the others flit around it like millers around a street-light.

A doctrinal sermon is not in a class all by itself as a type of sermon and thus to be distinguished from other types of sermons such as topical, textual or expository. Either of these three types may be a doctrinal sermon. It all depends on the Scriptural basis of the sermon. If the Scriptural text is part of the broad stream of Divine self-revelation, the sermon will be doctrinal in atmosphere, flavor and teaching. If the Scriptural basis is practical, hortatory, consolatory or such like, the classification of topical, textual and expository stands. As sure as these three types of sermons are truly Biblical, thus certainly will they even as such administer now and then a salutary doctrinal injection.

No church can live without doctrinal preaching. But Christian people generally do not react favorably to the idea of doctrinal preaching. They regard it as dry, irrelevant, old-fashioned, heavy, uninteresting. Why such a reaction? One weighty reason is apt to be the failure to preach Christian doctrine thematically and to adhere to the true sermonic form. A doctrinal sermon is not necessarily the sermonic presentation of a whole doctrine. It is in the first place a thematic sermonic presentation of the doctrinal significance of a chosen Bible verse or passage. If a preacher undertakes to present the doctrine of God in one sermon, the truth will be like a large container of powdered egg or milk, very dry. But take the aspect of the doctrine as seen from the angle of one verse or clause or even a paragraph and the sermon can be like a lovely "fried egg sunny side up." The thematic sermonic form makes one sermon one concentrated beam of light. Just as the moon, shining on the sea on a clear night, opens a highway of light to far horizons, so a thematic doctrinal sermon turns a truth-laden Bible verse or passage into a searchlight which penetrates dark lands beyond the sea and ministers to the homesickness of the soul. No Christian can have a healthy spiritual life without listening regularly to thematic doctrinal preaching. This is the type of preaching which enables a Christian to "grow in the grace and in the knowledge of our Lord and Saviour Jesus Christ." Doctrine is food but who can eat a whole cow all at once? Doctrine is medicine but who can stand an overdose? God's truth is food and medicine, but a thematic doctrinal sermon is dosage without dotage.

Even if the doctrinal preacher adheres to the thematic sermonic form he must qualify himself in the art of realistic exposition, description and portrayal, as well as in the art of apt illustration. Failure here is bound to result in aridity. The truth of God has to be real to a preacher if he is to make it real to his people. It can only be real to him if he exposes his soul to it, drinks it in and lives on it and by it. No one can say what this will cost a minister. World conditions make it imperative for Christians and for preachers especially to be out and out for God and so to live that there can be no shadow of a doubt about the preacher's complete consecration to his task. A preacher who spends more time smoking than praying, who specializes more on cards and golf than on Christian scholarship, is under an awful handicap and exposed to indictment for turning the prophet's office into a job. There is absolutely nothing low about "the high calling of God in Christ Jesus" and a preacher's life has everything to do with his preaching. A professor of preaching ought not necessarily to expose himself to the charge of totalitarian dictatorship, when he broods over his brethren in the ministry and ministers still in the making, with loving longing that they will be in the world yet not of it, giving Christ "the last full measure of devotion," becoming even "smokeless wonders" for His sake Who gave His all. At a time when worldliness is daring, blatant and lawless, when ordinary decencies and divine moral imperatives are carelessly trampled under foot and future harvests of present low standards are being sown with lavish hand, part of a preacher's task is to show by life as well as lip, that Jesus satisfies, that Christ is all and that the joy of salvation leaves no hankering for the life which was forsaken when "Jesus came in to stay."

As to the art of illustration in thematic doctrinal preaching, every preacher cultivates an open eye for the hand of God in daily life and in daily occurrences the wide world over. A famous novelist wrote in one of his books that love is not blind, it is an extra eye which sees the good. So love for Christ and for souls opens a preacher's eyes to the eternal spiritual significance of temporal occurrences. A preacher's love for his people, his love in Christ for them, creates a paternal brooding for their soul's welfare, so that he is always on the alert for everything that may be baptized, as it were, in the name of the Father and of the Son and of the Holy Spirit, for sermonic uses. A "live" Christian preacher is always sharpening arrows, has developing eyes for arrows in the making and studies to show himself approved in sermon illustration, a workman who need not be ashamed, whose illustrative power never violates thematic proprieties. When he reads of one, now a prison warden, qualifying his legally innocent self for his future office by having himself incarcerated in jail as a criminal and living the life of one apparently under just retribution, in order to learn the inner life of the prisoners he was to superintend, he will sense that he is on the threshold of a first-class illustration for his forthcoming sermon on the incarnation of Jesus Christ. One of the favorite hymns of a thematic doctrinal preacher is, "Open my eyes that I may see." A preacher must be able to see in order to tell. In all dark areas of human confusion, he is the man who sees.

Suppose a preacher selects John 3:16 as the basis of a doctrinal sermon. "For God so loved the world, that He gave His only begotten Son, that whosoever believeth on Him should not perish, but have eternal life." This is a verse rich in doctrine: the doctrine of God, of the world, of the Person of Christ, of the Work of Christ, of faith, of hell and of eternal life. One cannot give prominence to all these doctrines in one sermon. But they can all be touched upon in one doctrinal sermon without doing violence to the principle of unity. The preacher decides whether he will give the main stress to the wonderful love of God and make that the subject and essence of a theme or whether he will preach the text in terms of eternal life and make the other doctrines contributory to the concept of eternal life.   He might wonder whether the text can best be preached in terms of the only begotten Son. Whatever the choice, only a thematic sermon is going to put over a unified message.   Experimenting in theme construction from every possible standpoint warranted by the text will have much to do with final choice of which doctrine is to have preeminence in discussion.

A first try might be made with a theme like this: "God's love in Christ provides a free salvation" or "God's love in Christ puts eternal life within reach." Take the second suggested theme: God's love in Christ puts eternal life within reach.   In John 3:16, it is hard to get away from the apparent priority of eternal life.   It is legitimate, however, to feel that it is God's love which is stressed.   "God" is the subject and "loved" is the first verb.   The ideal development of a theme is its development in terms of one term or word in the theme. Do it now in terms of the term "God's Love."   Division I could be, The Genesis of God's Love.   Division II. The Gift of God's Love.   Division III.  The Goal of God's Love. The word "Genesis" in Division I and the word "gift" in Division II may not be too ideal, but you are always lured by a possible alliteration, knowing that it will be easier for the people to remember, to say nothing of the preacher's memory.

What is in one preacher's mind may not be in another preacher's mind.   Must one therefore justify the three divisions?   Inasmuch as the choice is to proclaim God's wonderful love in a doctrinal sermon on John 3:16, it is proper to look at that love of God. It is said, "God so loved the world." Now why should God love "this world"?  To be sure, "it is He that hath made us" but it is the world which turned rebel and lives in defiance and contempt of God.   One might find grounds to say that there is no reason in what men are by nature for a holy and righteous God to love such a world.   Love is usually brought to life and nurtured by some quality or qualities in the loved one.  What is there in a self-centered, secularized and vulgarly egoistic mankind for God to love?

It is evident that in preaching on John 3:16 in terms of God's wonderful love, the Christian view of this world as a perishing world, because it is a corrupt world, is going to serve as Background.  The whole thing is clear at once and it might as well be said at once.  There is no doubt about it that John 3:16 exhibits the wonderful love of God.  The verse brings before us three gigantic facts which make God's love stand out like the infinite wonder it is.  The first fact is what a theologian has called "this damned human race," this rebel race, this sinning, dying perishing world.  The more you appreciate the enormity of man's sin, the more God's love will stand out in immeasurable stature.  The second fact is the unspeakable gift of God's Son.  Only a far deeper and vaster appreciation of our adorable Saviour Jesus Christ will give us a truer realization of the marvelous love of God.  The third fact is the astonishing prize God dangles before the eyes of a perishing world, free for the asking, free, that is, for those who will own up to their bankruptcy before God, abdicate from self-management and jump into the arms of the Everlasting Mercy.  At this point, a preacher can dig up an old "Moody and Sankey Hymn Book" and turn to the hymn, "God loved the world of sinners lost, And ruined by the Fall: Salvation full at highest cost, He offers free to all."  The chorus will stick with you for days, "O, 'twas love, 'twas wondrous love, The love of God to me; It brought my Saviour from above, To die on Calvary."  It is evident that John 3:16 is a suitable text for a doctrinal sermon on "God's Measureless Love" and that Division I on the Genesis of God's love is quite in point by clearest implication when you take it in that it is human society apart from Jesus Christ, this sin-stricken, devil-ridden world which God loved.  You ask, "What reason is there for God loving this bad world?"  The answer is, "God loves this world because God is love."  The reason is not "in the World" but in God Himself.  When God all-holy so loved such a world you have a great love to preach about.

Division II on "The Gift of God's Love" will discuss the love of God in terms of the love of the man Christ Jesus, not forgetting the love of God that gave but seeing God's love in action in Christ, noting how holy the love of God is, how self-sacrificing and self-giving, how full of grace, being a love for sinners, that is, for such as do not deserve it.  The doctrines of the Person and Work of Christ, so clearly implied in the text, serve thus as background to expound the love of God. The discussion under Division II will set forth not only the love that gave Christ, but the size and significance of the living gift as well, as a measure of God's love, not excluding to what this only begotten Son of God was given — to self-emptying, humiliation, suffering and crucifixion.

Division III on the Goal of God's Gift will expound the eternal life which God has made available in Christ.  "Salvation full at highest cost, He offers free to all."  Bring in Bryant's "Thanatopsis."  Remind yourself that "all that tread the earth are but a handful to the tribes that slumber in its bosom."  Reflect on the sway of lordly death.  Imagine the earth as a universal cemetery.  "The paths of glory lead but to the grave."  This world is a perishing world.  In such a world God's love is in action to redeem, to save, to deliver, to communicate God's own true Divine life through our Saviour Jesus Christ.  God's love provides escape from death and the grave.  Here you bring in the last great enemy Death in order to show that we are "more than conquerors through Him Who loved us."  How matchless is God's love when considered against the background of the badness of man, the grace of the Saviour and the priceless boon offered to faith in Christ.

The theme suggested, "God's love in Christ puts eternal life within reach" may seem to need revision from the standpoint of the divisions.  A theme should contain the divisions of the sermon-body either by direct statement or evident implication.  Is it necessary to make the theme longer, like this, "God's love in Christ puts eternal life within reach of a perishing world"?  The four words, "of a perishing world" could be reduced to three by saying "of lost sinners." The four are stronger than the three from the standpoint of stressing eternal life. "Eternal life to a perishing world" is an immense idea. The words, "of lost sinners," is stronger than the words "of a perishing world" from the standpoint of stressing God's love. Sinners do not deserve God's love. To say, therefore, that God's love in Christ offers eternal life to sinners or brings eternal life within reach of sinners, is to imply that the origin or genesis of God's love must be elsewhere than in the bad world God loved. A preacher can go on in this way, thinking, writing, praying, reading, studying, reconsidering, looking at the matter from every conceivable angle, always by all these ways deepening insight, understanding, power to think, facility and felicity of expression, building background, growing in Christian knowledge, increasing redemptive atmosphere and gaining in preaching power.

If the suggested theme be retained, may it not be argued that the words "of a perishing world" or "of lost sinners" can be regarded as truly implied? The words "within reach" certainly mean within reach of "the world" which the text views as perishing. The first division, "The Genesis of God's love" means to say that God loved the world because God is love. God's love has in a sense no "genesis," but common sense understands the language. When God's love is said to originate in Himself, it does not mean that God's love had a beginning, but that it is an expression of His nature. The text is proof of God's love like Romans 5:8. One might feel that it cannot be taken for granted that God loves a rebel world. If God does love a world which turned against Him, a proper question would be, "How does God happen to love such a world?" To credit God with loving an evil world is no easier when one reflects that "the wrath of God is revealed from heaven against all unrighteousness of men." The whole atmosphere of the text is that love in God for such a world as this needs proof and explanation. The first division on "The Genesis of God's Love" is therefore in harmony with text and theme. Love in God for a sinful, perishing world gets right down to what kind of a God the Supreme Being of the universe really is. God's love, it is implied, originates in Himself, that is, is part of His Being, is, in fact, the total essence of His being. It is thus eternal rather than originated, but the word "genesis" serves to focus thought on what God really, essentially and eternally is. The theme means that "God shows what He is by giving Christ as Saviour." You are about ready to do nothing but speak thematically. What God is, is shown by what Christ was and did for sinners. God proves His love for the world by giving the world a Saviour. Keep on with thought and sentences like these. One who does so is headed for the simplicity which marked the preaching of Jesus.

Objections to the thematic suggestions for the sermonic treatment of John 3:16 herein made may all be worthy. No one preacher is perfect. But a preacher has a great task. He does big business when he prepares and delivers a sermon. When his text is doctrinal, he touches the stars, the moon and the sun in the sky of God's redeeming grace. Get the best theme possible. Make it simple. Honor the doctrine you wish to stress in the theme and divisions. Make theme and divisions revolve around it. It takes work. It takes prayer. It can and ought to and must be done.

# XIV

## Thematic Narrative Preaching

THE Bible is the story of a Divine crusade of redemption. It is a history of God's interposition in human affairs. It is a record of events which have to do with God's introduction of His kingdom among men. It therefore treats of persons individually, in groups and in the larger units of nations. As an historical record the Bible is full of narratives, stories of persons, families, nations and events. The narrative element is a rich harvest field for the preacher. The stories of the Bible have conspicuous preaching values. One of the most interesting types of sermon is the narrative sermon, the presentation of a story of the Bible in sermon form.

In all types of preaching, the sermonic form must be stressed. A preacher is not a story-teller by profession, but a preacher, both by profession and by the call of God. What he presents in the pulpit must be a sermon with theme and divisions, a specific form of oral presentation of Bible truth and teaching, calculated to be a unified message aimed at a definite goal. The Bible story of a person or event may teach a fundamental truth of God's redemptive interest in man. If a preacher chooses to use such a story as the basis of a sermon, it will most effectively serve his purpose if he uses it in thematic sermonic form.

Two types of narrative sermons have been distinguished. One was brought to eminence by an outstanding American preacher of the nineteenth century, William M. Taylor. He preached series of sermons on such matters as the parables and miracles of Jesus. His way of doing it was to tell the narrative first, in which this preacher had striking gifts of realistic portrayal, and then to add a number of lessons apparent in the narrative, for which he also had special competence. But why should a story publicly told, followed by a recital of pertinent lessons, be called a sermon, when a sermon is a very specialized form of oral presentation, marked first of all by one theme, expounded, illustrated, enforced and applied, in a balanced, symmetrical, progressive unified message?

The best type of narrative sermon is the thematic, in which the preacher labors to get to the heart of a Bible narrative in order to search out its fundamental significance. When he has arrived at a verdict, he puts himself under orders to express the chief lesson or significance of the narrative in a theme which embraces by direct statement or evident implication the aspects of it to be organized into sermonic form. The theme and the divisions are all to be stated in universal, timeless, yet contemporary form. The effort always is to present a timely message and a message is most timely when it is timeless, speaking what is always true for all people. Theme and divisions, therefore, must be stated in general terms, universally true, always applicable to the human situation, yet drawn from the narrative presented.

Suppose a preacher in his sermon preparation chooses to develop his theme along three lines. In narrative preaching such a decision is based on what the narrative yields. The narrative is to be told during the sermon but not at any one point or all at once. The divisions will have to do with stages of the story. During the development of a particular division, only so much of the narrative is to be related as is necessary to make the division or aspect of the theme intelligible. The progress of the Scripture story sets the standard for its telling as the sermon progresses. The stages of the story are incorporated into the appropriate stages or divisions of the sermon. But it is not necessary to tell the whole story about a person or event in a single narrative sermon. Only so much of the narrative is to be employed as is necessary for the development and exposition of the theme and the divisions. Thus it is truer to say that the requirements of the theme and divisions set the standard for drawing on the narrative. The story must be told in the measure that it is needed to justify the theme and the divisions. The narrative is always basic to the theme and divisions, but when once the narrative has yielded theme and divisions, the theme and divisions become the judge of how much of the narrative is to be presented in the sermon and at what divisional point.

It is best for the introduction of a narrative sermon to contain some arresting remarks about the subject and theme to be considered. It must then be stated that the subject and theme proposed are drawn from a Scripture narrative which is to be used in the course of the sermon. If the narrative contains a verse which expresses the essence of it and determines the theme, such a verse may be announced as the key-verse of the sermon. Do not use the word "text" in announcing the key-verse. A narrative sermon is not a thematic and sermonic presentation of the message of a key-verse, but of the whole narrative. To suggest a key-verse is in a sense an accommodation to a congregation accustomed to the idea of a text for every sermon. It offers in the key-verse a possible memory verse for the hearers. It must be made clear that the message is based on the entire narrative. If the narrative does not easily lend itself to a key-verse, the preacher may select a key-verse from any part of the Bible, never failing to state what story it is which is to undergird the sermon. A narrative may be too long to be used for a Scripture lesson in a service of public worship. If so, selected verses or paragraphs may be read, but care must be exercised in selection, topic and theme constituting a Board of Directors.

Theme and divisions of a narrative sermon are announced at the close of the introduction. Topic and narrative on which the sermon is based are announced just before beginning the introduction. After the introduction the first division is announced again, this time both rhetorically and logically and always in general terms. Then is given as much of the Bible story as is needed to present the first division of the theme. The Bible story is, of course, usually told in the preacher's own words. Here lies the danger of narrative preaching. The preacher must necessarily use his imagination. He has felt the permanent significance of the Bible narrative. He has seen into the heart of it and knows that it speaks to the life of today. He naturally wants to be realistic and impressive. But he must labor to keep within bounds. He must not let his imagination run away with him. He must keep the narrative parts of the sermon up to levels of dignity commensurate with Biblical standards. Liberty in narration can very easily become license. Slang is taboo. Language must at all times be kept chaste and refined, as well as simple and appropriate. A preacher cannot afford to make a mistake here. Low standards are absolutely forbidden. The pulpit is not a stage and preaching is not acting a part. It is Divine reality facing the tragedy of the plight of man.

When the necessary portion of the narrative has been told in the preacher's own words, it is time to give the contemporary interpretation and to put the matter in terms of present-day life. In explaining narrative preaching, it has been customary to say that in a narrative sermon the application is made in each division. This can easily be misunderstood and lead preachers to put as many conclusions in a narrative sermon as there are divisions. To interpret the word application in this connection as exhortation is an error. The meaning rather is the pointing out of contemporary parallels or situations which express today what the Biblical narrative expressed for the long ago. In showing the relevance for today of that part of the story told in any one division of the narrative sermon, care must be exercised not to tell other stories in detail. References may be made to illustrative parallels, but the parallels must not be described in the same way that the Biblical narrative is used. The Biblical story has the right of way and no competitive stories should be told. In that sense, illustrations are out of order in thematic narrative preaching. Contemporary parallels may be listed, referred to, and cited in witness of links in the present with the past, but the narrative preacher is not in his pulpit to spin yarns. His task is to preach the whole counsel of God, a great part of which is enshrined in the narrative portions of Scripture. The Scripture event which forms the basis of a thematic narrative sermon is the only story the sermon needs or ought to have. Each division has its appropriate part of the story, followed by exposition and interpretation of its contemporary and timeless significance against a background of pertinent present-day allusions.

When the second division is reached, it is announced both rhetorically and logically, just as the first division was. This is followed by continuing the Bible narrative in the preacher's own words, but only so far as the second division calls for a part of the narrative, that part, namely, which illustrates the second division. If there are three or even more divisions the same process is followed in each division. The order is: 1. Rhetorical and logical statement of a division. 2. The pertinent part of the Bible narrative. 3. The interpretation of the narrative in terms of contemporary life. Allusions to present-day parallels are in point, but not detailed delineation of some modern life or event. A narrative sermon contains one story, and that one story is the Bible story of an occurrence or a life.

It is conceivable that a preacher might want to preach a narrative sermon and use a life like that of D. L. Moody, for example, as a basis. That might work out very effectively. Where such a thing is attempted, the idea would be to select some Scripture verse or passage which might serve as a key-verse and to use the life of Moody without a Bible narrative. It may be that you read a little book called, *Why God Used D. L. Moody*. This quickened interest in fuller biographies of Moody. The result was a determination to present his life to your congregation in sermonic form. In such a sermon the theme and divisions would be drawn from the life of this man of God and each division would contain facts about Moody's life and work appropriate to the division. If use were made of Moody's habits of Bible study and prayer and of Moody's Spirit-filled life, such a sermon could be shot through with Bible references and so be made a truly Biblical sermon. If a text could be found in Scripture which would yield the same theme as the man's life, a preacher would be all set in harmony with the requirements of pulpit propriety. The history of the church has many illustrious names of men and of women, too, whose lives embody the power of the Word of God and demonstrate the promises of Scripture. Narrative sermons, thematically constructed to perpetuate the life and influence of such dynamic leaders, might be a vital part of a revival of pulpit power in America.

One life in one sermon is enough just as in other types of sermons one illustration of a point is plenty, if illustration is needed. A sermon should not be a bundle of stories or illustrations, any more than it should be a collection of varied thoughts. A sermon must take a congregation somewhere. In narrative preaching, the story is like a sight-seeing bus. There is plenty to see, if the preacher tells the story as he should, with fitting use of a sanctified imagination. A narrative sermon tells a story on the installment plan, telling the whole story if called for in as many installments as there are divisions, but telling it in sermonic form with a theme as the conductor of the sermonic tour.

Stories of the great hymns of the church and stories of the missionary enterprise of the Christian Church may likewise serve as inspiring fillers of thematic sermonic frame-work, but with only one hymn or enterprise per sermon. Bible narratives which contain the historical record of the redemption which is in Christ Jesus are worthy of constant telling in the form of thematic narrative sermons during the relevant seasons of the Church year. The story of the birth of Jesus, of the Baptism, the temptations, the transfiguration, the trial, the crucifixion, the resurrection and the ascension, all lend themselves fully to narrative sermon structure and give the preacher coveted and highly prized opportunity to preach the redemptive Gospel of Jesus Christ. No Bible story should be told merely as a story in pulpit ministry. It must be used with thematic sermon form as container and then the story constitutes significant content.

Narrative preaching has much to commend it. If ably done, it is very interesting. In a day when general ignorance of the

Bible over wide areas is nothing short of appalling, narrative sermons are fine techniques for spreading Bible knowledge and inducing people to become habitual Bible readers. A thematic narrative sermon is an effective vehicle for interpretation of Bible narratives. The sermonic form of thematic presentation insures a sense of message in the preacher. The preparation of a thematic sermon tends more and more to become a fine intellectual and spiritual experience as the preacher turns miner and digs out of Scripture precious diamonds of great lustre.

The principles of thematic narrative sermon structure may be specifically illustrated. Suppose you decide to preach a narrative sermon on the story of the interview of Jesus with the woman of Samaria recorded in the Gospel of John, chapter four. The subject would not be "Jesus and the Woman of Samaria." One writer on the Gospel of John considers the woman of Samaria a case of frustration. In his judgment, the story of Jesus' interview with her is a permanent message to the frustrated. The woman had had five husbands and at the time of her interview with Jesus was living with a man who was not her husband. She must have had personality and attractive qualities to attain a record of five marriages and the affair with the sixth looks like an effort to fight frustration. The interview of Jesus with this woman causes her to disclose her religious confusion. Up to the time of her interview with Jesus, she was evidently nowhere as far as the moral uses of life are concerned. She had tried and apparently exhausted the possibilities of her situation. It is here that Jesus comes into her life and lifts it out of its frustrations to heights of spiritual reality and testimony. The story shows the difference Christ makes. The last four words can serve as subject of a sermon, "The Difference Christ Makes" and the theme could be, "Christ has what it takes to change frustration into realization." Divisions could be: I. The Reality of Frustration. A life without Christ never gets anywhere. II. The Cause of Frustration. It just is not in any human being to make a go of it without Christ. III. The Cure of Frustration. One who accepts what Christ offers knows by experience that Jesus satisfies. Here are three divisions stated both rhetorically and logically.

Division I would require a portrayal of the woman's spiritual condition at the time Jesus met her at the well. The story must be searched for data. Her state was one of spiritual destitution and general frustration. She came to the well at the noon-hour when the day was at its hottest. She apparently came at that time in order not to meet anyone. People would naturally avoid going to a distant well at the most uncomfortable time of day. There was a reason for this woman going at a time when no one else went. With this as a starter, the preacher keeps probing into the story. She apparently was no longer human enough to give a thirsty man a drink on a hot day without bringing in the matter of racial and other social barriers. A listless, apathetic, do-not-care, indifferent kind of a woman! As far as heights of radiant living are concerned, this woman's life was very low. She could only think of well-water when Jesus was making supreme revelation of Himself as able to satisfy the thirst of the soul for God. She shows herself able to put up some kind of a religious argument, but in a way that shows her religion to be divorced from life. When Jesus said to her, "Ye worship that which ye know not," he clearly indicated the religious delusion which marked her life. Both the woman's religious confusion and her secular experience as revealed in the story show the reality of her frustration. It is apparent that the imagination must play an important role in telling the story of this woman's life as sketched with a few bold strokes. It may be added that a hard study of good commentaries and other pertinent literature will greatly aid the imagination to do a good job.

Division II will utilize Jesus' knowledge of this woman's life as a key to understanding the cause of her frustration. "Go call thy husband and come hither." "I have no husband." "He whom thou now hast is not thy husband." From this sordid depth, Jesus soars swiftly into the blue azure of true worship, but enough is swiftly indicated to tell of a full life still empty and of ways traversed without getting along. Great qualities of personality can be justly inferred, but her life seems to be involved in the total bankruptcy of total depravity and the wonderful Saviour is right there to tie her to an anchor of hope that holds within the veil. A preacher once said, "When a woman is good, she is ten times better than a man; when she is bad, she is ten times worse." The well of Jacob by which Jesus sat was very deep but not nearly as deep as that woman's sinful and guilty past. But neither "well of Jacob" nor deep-dark sins of the surprised woman were anywhere nearly as deep as the love of the Incarnate Son of God Who was right on the job to make all things new for that blasted and frustrated woman.

Division III addresses itself to the cure of her frustration. Go over the story again in your mind and see how soon Jesus is doing His Saviour business. Tell the relevant parts of the story in this division. "If thou knewest the gift of God, etc." "Whosoever drinketh of the water that I shall give him, shall never thirst." "I that speak unto thee am he." Tell her reactions. Tell how she forgot about her water-pot and how she ran to the village, not to avoid notice but to arrest it, not to carry water but to give testimony, showing that life's most wonderful experience had come to her. When she came to the well, frustration was written all over her. But when she "went to town" it was as an ambassador of Christ and when she returned to the well, it was in the spirit of the hymn, "We shall come rejoicing, bringing in the sheaves." What a day in her life, in the life of her village, in the life of Jesus! Frustration is written in letters of blood over the self-willed striving of millions. But Christ has what it takes to transmute frustration into realization and into achievement through testimony. "O happy day that fixed my choice, On thee my Saviour and my God; Well may this glowing heart rejoice, And tell its raptures all abroad. Happy day! Happy day! When Jesus washed my sins away."

It ought to be said that words like "frustration" and "realization" are big words for some folks in church. In the interest of brevity of theme, we allowed them to stand. If you can find simpler ones, use them. If not, explain them. Write a hundred different themes synonymous with this one: "Christ has what it takes to change frustration into realization." Here is one, "Christ has what it takes to undo the mischief of sin." Here is another, "Christ has what it takes to handle a bad past." Try your hand at it. If you get a better one than the one used, God may make you a professor of preaching, especially if you can produce divisions to match your theme.

The Old Testament prophets furnish excellent camping and stamping ground for the thematic narrative preacher. Try it, for example, on such a prophet as Hosea. He learned great lessons of God in terms of personal and domestic experience. He married a remarkable woman and he must have had splendid qualities himself to get her. But the life of a prophet's wife proved too tame for her. What a story for the power of a holy imagination! Hosea's love persisted in spite of his wife's unfaithfulness. She went from bad to worse and was at last sold into the slavery of prostitution. Hosea bought her and brought her back with a love that never died, with a love that would not let her go. Then his eyes were opened to see that his own situation with reference to his wife was a symbol of God's relation to Israel. God was the Husband of His people Israel. Israel was like a faithless wife. But God in mercy always redeemed His apostate people. Here is a somewhat crude and too long first attempt at a theme for a thematic narrative sermon on the entire book of Hosea, "Man's rebellion against God involves him in ruin, but God in love persists in redeeming." The theme has three key words: rebellion, ruin, redemption. The subject could be: "The Challenge Of God's Love." Smooth it out, who will. Narrative sermons, thematically constructed, can be fine techniques for preaching the doctrines of the prophets.

The possibilities of thematic narrative preaching on the parables will be shown in a demonstration sermon on the parable of the Prodigal Son. A single parable does not teach the whole redemptive Gospel. One must pay the price of qualifying himself to decide what the main import of a parable is. Would

you say that the parable of the Prodigal Son teaches fundamentally "God's Readiness To Forgive?" The atonement is
not in this parable, but God's forgiving love is. Judge for
yourself how near the sermon comes to hitting the bull's eye.
The demonstration sermon is risky business, because of the
use made of the imagination. Who has made a professor of
preaching a law-giver? To err is human but a professor of
preaching hopes for the best.

A very gifted preacher on occasion preached a narrative
sermon in the first person, putting himself in the place of a
Bible character. He preached such a sermon, for example on
Nicodemus. His first sentence was, "My name is Nicodemus."
Then he gave an imaginary portrayal of Nicodemus, with himself as Nicodemus. He recounted not only the events of Nicodemus' life, as these are reflected in Scripture, but his moods
and reactions in the spheres of the intellectual and religious.
Lacking text, theme and divisions, it was not really a sermon
but it was unforgettable, living in the memory of one who
heard it for nearly fifty years. If a duly competent preacher
could do that thematically in sermonic form, he could be
mightily used of God in an age when a crying need is preachers
who "go to town" when they preach.

# XV

# Thematic Sermon Delivery

T HE best formula for sermon delivery as far as voice and tonal quality are concerned is contained in the two words "animated conversation." To shout and yell in preaching affects the nervous system of a hearer like the honking of an automobile horn when you cannot get the horn to stop. Preaching is proclamation but not declamation. One senses the difference between the two. The former has the importance of things which make a difference; the latter beguiles a passing period.

A preacher talks to his people when he preaches but what he says is a matter of life and death. It must make a difference to a preacher that what he says is so important. His feeling of its significance produces the animation.

Experience and realization are the best courses in elocution. When a lad has seen a circus parade he is soon making his plea to his mother to take him to the circus. He is all animation. He has seen the lions, tigers, bears, and elephants. "O please, mother, let me go to the circus." But his mother reminds him of his disobedience and says, "I do not think I can let you go to the circus." His animated conversation may now become bathed in tears punctuated with sobs and renewed appeals. He sees his mother wavering. He feels her softening. He becomes a school of elocution on the spot. He promises all due obedience from now on and forever. Presently he has permission and you ought to see him now. His happiness is eloquent beyond words. He rushes out to tell his pal who also has just rushed out to tell his pal, after the same kind of encounter with his mother. Listen to those boys and follow them to the circus if you want to see the source and techniques of eloquence.

The right kind of sermon delivery comes from within the preacher. He has to feel his message. He must get that sermon into his soul as well as into his mind. The truth as it is in Jesus must become personal realization. A preacher has to have his own heart warmed. Then he will not be able to act like a wooden Indian. When Paul Revere put in his great night, what he said was proclamation. When school boys tell about it, it is declamation. "Listen, my children and you shall hear, of the midnight ride of Paul Revere." Just so, just so. Everyone knows what a declamation is. But a preacher is a Paul Revere. He is one sent to cities of destruction to announce the perils of its citizens and to proclaim the acceptable year of the Lord, that is to say, deliverance. He must talk loud enough to be heard but not so loud as to break eardrums. If he keeps yelling, even Paul Revere will get so hoarse as to be unable to talk above a whisper. "Animated conversation" is the preacher's formula for sermon delivery. He has to be alive and lively and not a dead one, but everything must be under control. It is what a preacher is as a Christian, as a man of God, as a Spirit-filled man, as one living in the experience of an up-to-date salvation and as one who realizes in his own soul the grace, the presence and the power of Christ, that qualifies him for "animated conversation" in pulpit sermon delivery.

As to articulation, "speak plainly, if you speak at all. Carve every word before you let it fall." But be careful, at that, in this business of carving words. Follow the ancient Greek motto, "Nothing to excess." You want to be heard. You ought to be heard. You must be heard or else. Speak so as to be heard by those in the last pew. That does not necessarily mean that you have to lift your voice and pitch it high if your natural voice is deeper down. Be natural unless it is natural for you to be unnatural. Unlearn your faults of speech. Gargle daily with salt water so as to keep the channels of speech clear of gathering frustrations. No use preaching if you cannot be heard. But even bad acoustics are no excuse for yelling. A call to preach does not include a call to yell. Preach so as to be heard, but never strain or violate your personality in preaching.

As to posture. Stand behind the pulpit desk with its open Bible before you. Some advocate moving from side to side of that desk. Suppose the church auditorium contains a loud speaking system? Where did anyone ever get that idea of walking around? Was a preacher ever called to be a perambulator? It is good counsel to stay put behind the pulpit desk. Fortunately the preaching desk in many great churches does not admit of a minister walking all over the pulpit platform. Do not lean on the desk. Do not spread yourself out over it. Try even to keep your hands off. Train them to hang where God put them. The physical organism of the preacher must be kept in abeyance. There must be nothing in the preacher's pulpit stance or behaviour to divert attention from his message. The idea of a pulpit gown and of a Prince Albert coat is to bury possible sources of distraction out of sight. Nose, throat, ears, eyes and glasses must receive all necessary attention before entering a pulpit. No shabbiness in dress or lack of shoe-shine is tolerable. The Gospel has priority. The story must be told and not hindered by the one man called to put it over.

Do not feel that you have to gesture. You may not be that kind of a man. Here is a good rule: Do not gesture if you can avoid it. If you are so filled and thrilled by the message that you simply have to make gestures, make them graceful but not excessive. A preacher does not gesture souls into the kingdom of God. It is the regenerating Word which is the Sword of the Spirit. Any preacher who is forever gesturing and gesticulating ought to take himself in hand and cut it out. One who never gestures may lack a living message. Such a preacher ought to look into it. If it is not in a preacher to gesture, why should he gesture? Let such an one examine himself to discover how it is that he can preach without gesturing. Let a preacher give care to the spiritual dynamics of animation. He will simply have to make a gesture now and then to keep normal. But if he makes too many, that too is a fault. Who wants to see arms flying around in the pulpit without a let-up?

Thematic Christian preaching makes for correct, proper and effective sermon delivery. It organizes the preacher's personality and promotes the same unity in himself that he labors to inject into his sermons. If he says, "This one thing I do" in sermon preparation and construction, he will be properly motivated to do the same one thing in his delivery. Preachers like all moderns are inclined to spread themselves out "too thin" and to suffer from what a word-coiner called "scatteratiousness." Thematic Christian preaching is calculated to put the Christian preacher right "on the beam" in thought, word and deed. Get on the beam in what you preach. It follows as the night the day, you will be more and more on the beam in "delivering" the goods. Presently you will be reading books on voice culture. Thematic Christian preachers are great readers. They specialize on both "goods" and "delivery."

# PART TWO

## DEMONSTRATION SERMONS

Expository
Topical — Usual Form
Topical — Special Form
Textual
Doctrinal
Narrative

# XVI

## A Thematic Expository Sermon

### Christian Security

*Who shall separate us from the love of Christ?*

—ROMANS 8:35

I S IT possible for a Christian to be sure he is saved? Is there reason to feel insecure, to fear that at last one may lose out or miss salvation? Is there room for doubt? One who asks such questions would be wise to learn the eighth chapter of the epistle to the Romans by heart. It has to do with the security of the Christian. Paul gives seven reasons or grounds for the security of believers.

Paul's first reason for Christian security is the Christian's deliverance from condemnation. Sinful and guilty as man is before God, if he is united to Christ by faith, he is free from condemnation. This escape from condemnation is made possible by the sacrifice of Christ.

The second reason for Christian security is the believer's possession of the Holy Spirit which means that the power of God is at work in his life. The fact that God Himself is at work in a believer is a sure basis for confidence.

The third reason for Christian security is that a Christian is a member of the redeemed family of God. Paul speaks of him as a son of God, an heir of God and co-heir with Christ. No one could expect a child of God to have anything to worry about.

The fourth reason for Christian security is what God does for us in the troubles of life. It is shown that these are very trivial when compared with the glory in store for us. We are given a spirit of hope to tide us over and the Holy Spirit prays for us in a remarkable way. God makes everything work together for good. If every knock is a boost, why worry?

The fifth reason for Christian security is the purpose of God, the sovereign, predestinating purpose of God. Our present interest in Christ shows that God has started with us and He will finish what He began.

The sixth reason for Christian security is God's gift of His Son to be our Saviour. If God did not spare the supreme gift, there is no doubt that He will freely give us all things.

The seventh reason for Christian security is the love of God in Christ Jesus, a love which will last forever, from which nothing can separate us.

If Paul were speaking to a Christian who lacked assurance, he would say: "Not only have you nothing to worry about, but you have every reason to feel secure. God has freed you from the guilt of sin. God has come into your life with His blessed Holy Spirit. God has made you His child, a member of His family and an heir of all He has. God looks after you in times of trial. God has purposed from eternity to save you. God gave His own Son to die for you. God's love for you is unchangeable."

With Paul as our teacher we present as our theme that those who turn from self to Christ are forever secure in Him. Such is the position of the Christian in his relation to God and the striving creation that he is absolutely safe for time and eternity. Such are the possessions of a Christian that he will have always all sufficiency under all circumstances. Such are the eternal prospects of a Christian that what he has to endure in this present evil world is as nothing compared to his coming glory. We said purposely: "Those who turn from self to Christ." The blessedness of the Christian life is ours by faith. We own up that in ourselves we are helpless, bankrupt, without resource. We turn to Christ. We trust in Him. We put everything in His hands. We surrender to Him and give Him the reins. Those who thus turn from self to Christ are forever safe in Christ. They are secure now and forever.

Look first at the content of the Christian life as set forth in this wonderful chapter and see that such a life is forever secure.

Look next at the conflicts, the seeming contradictions, the crises in the life of a Christian and note what God does to support a Christian in trial as proof that God evidently intends to see a believer through to his destined glory.

Look finally at the culmination or consummation of Christian life in this world and see that such culmination and consummation involves its own continuance forever and ever.

We consider first the content of the Christian life as Paul sets it forth. To be a Christian is to be delivered from condemnation. It takes the joy out of life to be under condemnation. It is unpleasant to be condemned by anybody. What chance has a person if God condemns him? It is God with Whom we have to do. Our sins stand between God and us until they are forsaken and confessed and forgiven. Christ bore our sins in His body on the tree. Faith in Christ unites us to Christ and in Him we escape condemnation. By our faith in Jesus Christ we gain a verdict of acquittal. What can we do if God has anything against us? Christ took our sins upon Himself and bore them away on Calvary's Cross, so that "there is therefore now no condemnation to those who are in Christ Jesus." Because of what Christ has done for us and our trust in Him, we are freed from guilt. All charges against us are dismissed. We are cleared. God is on our side. He is for us because we are in Christ. You feel like shouting, "Hallelujah" when you think of it.

> *Bearing shame and scoffing rude,*
> *In my place condemned He stood;*
> *Sealed my pardon with His blood;*
> *Hallelujah! What a Saviour!*

You do not tell all it means to be a Christian when you say that there is now no condemnation to them who are in Christ Jesus. Precious as it is to be freed from the burden of guilt and to realize, as it is expressed in James Moffat's translation, that there is now no doom to a Christian, there is more to being a Christian than that. We may even say that the fact of no condemnation, no doom, is but the negative side of being a Christian. Positively, a Christian has entered on a new life and has a new life principle within him. "For the law of the Spirit of life in Christ Jesus hath made me free from the law of sin and death," says Paul. This is to say that a Christian is in possession of the Spirit of God. God Himself is personally present and at work in a believer's heart. Without the indwelling Spirit of God, we would have no interest in Christ. It is only by an act of God, through the Spirit, that we are united to Christ by faith and that we live and move "not after the flesh but after the Spirit."

It is a great thing that the Christian life proceeds from the Spirit of God. Paul clearly shows that it is not in man as he is by nature to be spiritually minded. The Son of God Who became man showed in his human life what God intended when He made man. The man Christ Jesus condemned sin in the flesh, that is, showed by His own sinless life that human life need not be sin-controlled, but may be God-controlled. Christ thus perfectly fulfilled all the requirements of God's laws. Christ lived our human life like a son of God. He *was* the Son of God and lived like one. He went further than to do what God required. He laid down that sinless life for the sins of the world. He offered it in our behalf, in our interest and in our place. The Spirit of God enlightens us as to all this. The Spirit of God opens our eyes to see Christ as our sin-bearing Saviour. The Spirit of God begets faith in the believer and a new life which changes him from being carnally minded to being spiritually minded. The Holy Spirit unites the believer to Christ and creates in him life by the Spirit. With such a life and with God Himself giving it, the Christian is entitled to feel secure.

It is further brought out that those who are thus guided by the Spirit of God are sons of God. The Holy Spirit makes the believer a child of God. A Christian is a member of the redeemed family of God. Every family on earth has its own atmosphere and language. In the life of a family words have meanings which are not found in the dictionary. Moreover, words are in use, pet names and loving expressions, which are not in the dictionary either. So Christians who are members of God's family learn to speak and to understand the language of the family. They get the real spirit of children of God. They are able to pray to God in a child-like spirit and they learn to call God "Father" as real children of God should. As sons of God it follows that Christians are heirs of God and co-heirs with Jesus Christ. It is simply unthinkable that God will let His children perish or that what he means them to have will never be theirs. All this is sure ground for security. If we are accepted in Christ and made sons of God and heirs of God with Christ, if this is what God Himself has done for us in Christ and in us by the Holy Spirit, it is evident that one who turns from self to Christ is safe in Christ forever. He is secure and will never fail of God's goal for human life.

Consider, secondly, the conflicts of the Christian life, the troubles and trials a Christian has to contend with, and learn that these are not inconsistent with our position and possessions and prospects in Christ and in no way militate against the security of the believer. The apostle here shows that what a Christian suffers in this world is trivial when compared with his eternal prospects. It is shown how these sufferings are a part of a universal striving toward the Divine goal of creation. This sin-cursed earth is the scene of a Divine crusade of redemption. God is at work undoing the mischief of sin and the whole creation is striving toward God's redemptive goal. God is in control of the human situation. Upon everything is impressed a law of work. God's aim for sinful men is something so gloriously immense and so immensely glorious that a terrific universal striving is involved in both man and creation moving steadily toward their destined goal.

Suffering in the Christian life is a necessary part of the process of our perfecting. God deals with us on moral principles. It is clearly brought out in the first part of the chapter

that salvation is holiness. Our natural tendency is to conceive
of salvation in terms of physical well-being and material prosperity. God has an eye on what can be made of us morally and
spiritually. His dealings with believers contemplate their growing likeness to Jesus Christ. God does not hesitate to disturb
us when we incline to run away from the struggle for spiritual
mastery and seek security in temporal things. It is interesting
to remember how it is said of Abraham, the great pioneer of
faith, that he dwelt in tents. Man's disposition is to build man-
sions of stone and to build as if he can stay here forever. But
we are pilgrims who have no continuing city in this present
life and this present world. We are never permitted for long
to seek final rest here. A tent is the fitting symbol of our stay
in this world. We are on the way to God's destined goal
of glory.

The apostle shows how all things are part of a system and
that the totality of things works for good to those who love
God and who are the called according to His purpose. Christians are informed that all things work together for good.
This thing or that which happens to us and strikes us as an
all but mortal blow may, by itself, constitute an appalling evil,
but God embraces it in His purpose for good and unites it
with everything else that happens to us and brings it about
that it all works out for our good in the long run. It is important to remember this "togetherness" of things. The single
experience may well-nigh overwhelm, but God makes it contribute to the goal of good together with the total experiences
of the Christian life.

It is also told us that the present life is built on the principle of hope. Once get the idea that this life is a preparatory
school to our perfected life in heaven and that all things, including the conflicting, contradictory and critical things in
Christian life which seem so inconsistent, help us on to the
glory, and it is evident that we are saved by hope. We could
not hold out, were it not for our prospects in Christ. As it
is we may sometimes get so low in spirit as to be unable
to lift up the head, but Paul assures us that the Holy Spirit

maketh intercession for us with groanings which cannot be uttered. This intercession is in harmony with the will of God and thus surely effective. Not only do we possess the Holy Spirit but the Holy Spirit possesses us and keeps us in the will and love of God. Suffering, therefore, is not inconsistent with our sonship to God. It does not endanger our spiritual security. It means that God is going on with us, that He means to bring us through. Suffer as we may and struggle as we must, we are forever safe in Christ.

Consider, finally, the possible culmination or consummation of Christian blessedness in the present which is the pledge and guarantee of its eternal permanence. The apostle realizes that the mature essence of the Christian life is oneness with Christy. He realizes that it was the eternal purpose of God to produce a race of men to whom He could give Himself in full measure and who through union with Christ would live in communion with God. God's sovereign purpose from eternity was to take all the steps necessary to conform believers to the image of Jesus Christ, to unite them in fellowship with His adorable Son. Whereas in his earlier life the apostle had faced the horror of condemnation, he now in his mature Christian life contemplates the possibility of being separated from the love of God in Christ Jesus. God has given him in Christ a great life, a life of inspired thinking, a life of exalted and rapturous feeling and a life of gloriously dynamic action and achievement. But suppose it comes to an end?

Bodily weakness, of course, foretokened physical death. The apostle knew that physical death would not deprive him of the goal. He triumphantly says, "But if the Spirit of Him that raised up Jesus from the dead dwelleth in you, he that raised up Christ Jesus from the dead shall give life also to your mortal bodies through his Spirit that dwelleth in you." He thinks of possible things that may separate him from the love of Christ. He is sure God is for him and for every Christian believer. He knows that God will not stop with partial ful-

filment of His purpose. Already God had foreknown and fore-
ordained and called and justified. He Who had done so much
would also glorify and finish what He had begun. Paul thinks
of God's gift of His Son, the supreme sacrifice of God for a
world of lost sinners and he regards this as evidence that
God will with Him freely give us all things.

"Who shall separate us from the love of Christ?" he says.
Christ of course is on the right hand of God making intercession
for us. But down here on this earth, in these storm-swept
lives of ours, there are factors of possible separation. Paul
goes over the list as he has experienced them. Tribulation,
anguish, persecution, famine, nakedness, peril, sword. He asks,
"Did these separate me from the love of Christ?" He remem-
bers how all these things promoted his fellowship with Christ,
accentuated his oneness with Christ, served to bring out the
nearness and reality and preciousness of Christ. All these con-
trary, seemingly inconsistent things, which swept over him
like billows on a stormy sea, seemed to be fresh avenues of
approach for Christ. He has come to see that his salvation
comes out of the wonderful love of God in Christ Jesus. God
has taught him in terms of his troubled and triumphant experience that the love of God is infinite and unchangeable.
The love of God which is in Christ Jesus our Lord is the fontal
source of a Christian's security. One who turns from self to
Christ is forever safe in Christ for "Jesus Christ is the same
yesterday, today and forever."

No, says Paul, it is not what we have to suffer which sep-
arates from Christ. Sin is the only separator. This rude self-
will of man is the dangerous thing. But in Christ all *that* has
been dealt with. God in Christ has bridged the chasm between
the sinner and Himself. The Divine provision covers the situation completely. We are eternally secure. We need never
worry. Our part now is to pray for the realization of salvation,
to yield to Christ the obedience of our faith, to give the indwelling Spirit full rights, to live in daily, trustful dependence and
in radiant hope and joy. "We are more than conquerors through

Him that loved us." The love of God will win because it lasts and is mightier than all opposition. "For I am persuaded that neither death, nor life, nor angels, nor principalites, nor things present, nor things to come, nor powers, nor height, nor depth, nor any other creature, shall be able to separate us from the love of God, which is in Christ Jesus our Lord."

# XVII

# A Thematic Topical Sermon — Usual Form

## The Fire of Jesus Christ

*I came to cast fire upon the earth; and what do I desire,
if it is already kindled?*                                    LUKE 12:49.

*I came to cast fire upon the earth; how would I that it were
already kindled!*          LUKE 12:49 (Marginal Reading)

C HRIST came to set the world on fire" said a wise commentator, "and the conflagration had already begun."
The Scripture chosen for the message gives us Jesus' own
word for it that he came to cast fire on the earth. Others have
had similar aim and the world has called them "firebrands."
The fires they started were out of line with the way of things
and either died down or were put out because the universe
was against them. The fire Jesus cast upon the earth is in
line with the way of things and is as indestructible as the im-
mutable laws of God.

Imagine a young man, just a little past thirty, in Palestine
and over nineteen hundred years ago, disclosing his sense of
mission, his dominant, passionate purpose in the words of our
text, "I came to cast fire upon the earth; how I wish that this
fire were already burning!" Jesus felt Himself to be under
the most solemn necessity of setting the world on fire in a
particular manner. The fact to remember about Jesus is that
He came and lived for the exclusive purpose of doing something about the sin of the world. It is not unusual now for
young people to dedicate themselves to the service of Jesus
Christ, to devote their lives either at home or abroad to win
souls for Christ and to build God's kingdom. But the astonishing ambition of Jesus was to do something about the totality
of human sin, to bear its penalty, destroy its power, cleanse

away its pollution and eradicate it as habit or character. It is the most stupendous purpose ever disclosed on earth. Any average person would be considered out of his head if he avowed it as his practical aim to deal sin a fatal blow which would continue operative and effective in defiance of time and which would inevitably insure the ultimate, final, complete and permanent undoing of sin for all who would avail themselves of what he would do about it. Just such an immense aim was in the mind of Jesus. He proposed, so to speak, to match wits with the powers of moral evil and he expected to come out on top. His soul was like a colossal volcano and he proposed to cast a fire on the earth which would never die down, which would go on generation after generation, burning the devil out of life and setting people on fire for God. His volcanic soul was intensely upheaved with this life mission of His and He was just burning up to get the fire going.

The subject for consideration is, "The Fire of Jesus Christ." The theme to direct thought may be expressed as follows: "Christianity is an indestructible fire kindled by Jesus Christ to save the world." Questions occur as follows: 1. In what sense is Christianity a fire? 2. What is the effect or result of Christianity as fire? 3. How is the fire of Christianity maintained? or, In what sense is it indestructible? Alternative questions are, What is this fire of Jesus Christ? What does it do? How does it keep on burning? We consider, first, the meaning of the fire of Jesus Christ; secondly, its effects and thirdly, its maintenance.

First, the meaning of the fire of Jesus Christ. The fire of Jesus Christ is what Jesus did about sin and for a sinful world on Calvary's Cross. It is the holy love of God expressed in the Divine self-sacrifice of Jesus Christ on the Cross. "Alas, and did my Saviour bleed, and did my Sovereign die?" Yes, sir, that is what happened on Calvary. God incarnate, God the Creator, "died for man, the creature's sin." "Amazing pity, grace unknown, and love beyond degree." The infinite and eternal love of the Supreme Being, the Supreme Moral Being of the Universe, came to a focus in the Cross of Christ, split open there, releasing energies which kindled a fire on earth never to be quenched. Christianity is an indestructible fire kindled by Jesus Christ to save the world.

Jesus knew that what it was in Him to do about the sins of the world would cost Him His sinless, matchless life. Only a holy love, pouring itself out in complete self-giving to the last full measure of perfect self-sacrifice and constituting God's full self-revelation in His suffering, dying, only-begotten Son, could start and be and keep going a fire to pierce the impenetrable hardness of man's impenitence and unbelief. The sin-bearing love of God came to atomic expression in the dying of Jesus for the sins of the world on the cruel Cross. There the volcanic heart of God's love poured out with ocean fulness the lava of regenerating grace. He Who brought the earth and the heavens to formed and orderly splendor out of primeval chaos, brooded over the evil heart of human corruption on Calvary's Cross with a redemptive heat that no resistance can finally stay.

Christ came to kindle regenerating and redeeming fires in the heart of man's rebellion. He kindled them by His sin-bearing love expressed in His death on the Cross. God was in Christ on that Cross putting all He is and has into the creation of a new humanity by redemption. All Divine saving powers latent in God were liberated on the Cross of Christ and sent like streams of fire down the years and into human hearts to burn up resistance and burn in the love everlasting. The fire of Jesus Christ is God's passion to redeem in action, putting forth the necessary expenditure of power and love and sacrifice to overwhelm and melt the hardness of human antagonism to God.

It is not without very special interest that Jesus uses the word "fire" to express the significance of His saving work, His dying on the Cross "as the one perfect sacrifice for sin." Fire is both a destructive and a constructive force. It consumes coal, wood, gas, oil or electricity and produces light, heat and power. The fundamental thing about fire is that the changes **it** effects are transmutations. When fire is done with a thing, the thing is gone, but only in the sense of having become something else, something other, something entirely new. Jesus came to send fire on the earth in all areas of man's rebellion against God. He came to send fire into the field of human self-management and all the dark regions of self-willed behaviour. He came to do something for and in a man which would transmute what was sin into holiness, what was rebellion into loyalty, what was self-willed into what is according to the will of God. Jesus Christ came to cast fire upon earth, to transmute hate into love, greed into self-giving, strife into peace, vulgar egoism into divine altruism, frustration into achievement, disintegration into realization. Jesus came to change what is wrong with the world into what expresses God's eternal purpose of grace. Nothing could possibly go deeper or as deep as the work of salvation undertaken by the Son of God in a sin-cursed, death-ridden world. Christ undertook to save a lost world not by force or violence but by the fire of a self-giving, all sacrificing and all-loving crusade of redemption.

What a place fire-arms have played in the history of man! Men have implemented fire in countless ways to achieve purposes of lust and greed or to stop the ravages of brutal despots. Fire, scientifically instrumented, has rained on hostile regions and forces, destroying human lives and values, sometimes with no regard to innocent and defenseless people and always to the hurt and death of those who love the ways of peace. When the fires of lust and greed rage in the souls of men, the best brains are regimented to give those internal fires technological implementation. The only answer man can make in such terrifying emergencies is to answer force with force, fire with fire, God giving strength to the nations which more nearly represent Him to call a halt to cohorts of savagery. But God's chief weapon in human reconstruction is the fire of His redeeming grace in Christ, the fire of His holy love, implemented by the Divine self-sacrifice in the death for sin on Calvary's Cross of the eternal Son of God. That Divine holy power of sacrifice is a fire of a new kind, designed to transmute what it destroys and to change secular passion into Christian enthusiasm. Only the most fundamental meaning of the word "fire" can serve to interpret the meaning of the fire of Jesus Christ which is the redeeming power of God liberated for human salvation by the Saviour of the world on the Cross of His sacrifice. The unheard of miracle of the incarnation and death of the eternal Son of God is God's full and final self-revelation as Redeemer as well as Creator of man. That saving deed wrought by Christ on the Cross as the God-man is the fire of an irresistible grace which burns the heart out of evil and transmutes it into praise and love of our Divine Redeemer.

Consider, now, the effect or result of Christianity as fire. What does the fire of Jesus Christ do? The fire of Jesus Christ produces the two extremely opposite results of transmuted life and on the other hand more determined antagonism and cleavage. Those in whom the fire of God's saving love in Christ makes all things new are not left to the joy and rapture of their salvation. The world erects a cross for them as it did for Christ. The fire which changes sinners into saints becomes in the redeemed a process, a perpetual fire consuming dross within and scorching evil in environment. The heart that has had the old nature burned out by the redeeming fire of Christ is now seen to be on fire for God and creeps over areas where the fires of man's self-will still rage. The result is persecution, crucifixion, often a living martyrdom. The fire of God's grace in Christ continues in a believer as a purifying fire, transmuting self-seeking into sacrifice and challenging others to submit and to expose their souls to the fire of Christ that saves.

The world and self do not take kindly to the fire of Jesus Christ. Being dead in trespasses and sin, the challenge of the fire of God's redeeming grace in Christ seems to a worldling to contain only a threat of destruction of all he prizes. He begins to specialize not only on defense mechanisms, but on counter-assaults, persuading himself that if he is to live, Christianity must die. So long has he been victimized by the despotism of lordly self, that power of moral discrimination is all but gone. He comes to a point where white looks black and truth is a lie. So long has he grieved and quenched and resisted the Spirit that the Spirit has ceased to strive with him. His state comes near to being what the New Testament calls the eternal sin, for which there is no forgiveness either in this world or the world to come, the blasphemy against the Holy Ghost. To fight against the fire of Jesus Christ does something terribly threatening to human nature, something that moves on to eternal destruction from the presence of the Lord. The battle line is clearly drawn between what the Bible calls "the children of light" and "the children of darkness." The children of light are full of the fire of Jesus Christ, the fire of His transmuting grace, the fire that steals from them into other lives, the holy fire of Christian testimony and enthusiasm. The children of darkness are full of the fire of self-centeredness, self-will, self-seeking, fire of lust and greed. So it transpires that the world is hard on its best people. It is blind to the things that pertain to its own peace. It chooses to hold out against God, to crucify the Son of His love, to start martyr fires for His people. Christ came to send fire on the earth, fire on the one hand that creates by destruction, but a fire, also, that the world hates with perfect hatred and seeks to stamp out at the cost of its salvation.

When the fire cast upon earth by the sacrifice of Christ on the Cross is seen for what it is as the unveiling and liberation of the holy and redeeming love of God, what that fire does in a believer is life's most wonderful experience. It blasts self out of the control room of personal life. It consumes the burden of one's guilt for sin in the fire of Divine forgiveness. It burns up all defilements and pollutions caused by the reign of sin. The fortress of sin's power goes up in flames. The corrupt heart is cleansed of false philosophies and turned into a sanctuary where the purified spirit worships Christ as Lord. Fires of redeeming grace destroy the cob-webs which prevent open vision in human personality. The holy fire of Christ's sacrificial death begets fire in the soul, the fire of inspired gratitude and living testimony as to salvation received.

The discovery that "the heart of the Eternal is most won-derfully kind," is a great experience. It makes everything just right when we know that God is on our side, by our side and effectively on the inside of us as Saviour all-glorious. The fire of Jesus Christ kindles all manner of fires in the believing heart, assuring a burning heart in a cold world. Whoever tries to warm himself exclusively by this world's fire is in for chilly days and nights. But at Calvary, molten lava of love, mercy and grace sweep over sin-laden souls to cement their everlasting union with Christ.

Who can measure what the fire of Christ has wrought on earth since the time it was kindled by the death of Jesus? Who can estimate the number of those who have been saved by the grace of Christ the Saviour? Who can compute the evil that has been burned out of human hearts by the cleansing fire of Christ's saving death? Measureless is the pardon, the peace, the purity, the power, which has come to numberless millions of Christian believers as the fire of Christ's sacrifice has trans-muted hearts of stone into hearts of flesh. Add to this every feature of life on earth and every factor in human society which owe their existence to God's love in Christ. The fire of Christian idealism consumes enough moral and physical evil to warrant optimism in times when reversion to paganism almost put an end to civilization. Homes of refuge, institutions of mercy, agencies of relief for distress, organizations embody-ing specific applications of the spirit of Jesus as well as the universal Christian Church and all of good sponsored by it declare trumpet-tongued the transforming and transmuting power of the fire of Jesus Christ. One who goes into it to see what Christ accomplished by His death on the Cross must conclude that the fire Christ cast upon earth has been an un-quenchable and indestructible source of the world's higher, bet-ter and true life. Such then is the effect of the fire of Jesus Christ. It transmutes sinful human nature into something new, making a believer a new man in Christ. It makes all things new for a Christian, changing everything, giving new life cen-ter but also a new risen life in Christ, changing human predi-

cament to the right to be called the children of God, guaranteeing maximum realization and expression in the sphere of
Christ's redemption.    It also creates cleavage, tension, strife,
persecution, suffering even unto death because of the blindness
and hostility of unregenerate man. But the fire of Jesus Christ
burns on, unquenched and indestructible, furnishing supernatural sustenance and inspiration to persevere unto the end of
man's evil because a believer can never get to the end of the
love that saved him.

Consider, finally, the maintenance of Christianity as fire
in answering the question, What keeps the fire of Jesus Christ
burning all over the world throughout successive generations
and down the years of personal life? God Himself keeps
the fire of His Divine self-sacrifice in Jesus Christ burning.
The fire of God's saving grace in Christ is indestructible
because the holy love of God for sinners is imperishable.
The love of God is eternal. It does not wear out. God
is love. Man can no more destroy God's love than he can
kill God. The world tried to get rid of Jesus by nailing
Him to a Cross but that foul deed of a depraved race only
split open the atomic bomb of God's redeeming grace in Christ,
liberating the fire that has raged ever since in destruction
of human depravity and transmutation of unnumbered sinners into children of God.

Christians, however, are challenged to keep near the fire
of God's love in Christ, to keep it in them by appropriate
action in order that it may increasingly burn out the bad and
burn in the good and thus make one's Christian life a holy
fire.  A missionary meant it for good when he expressed a
desire to burn out for God but the fire of Jesus Christ is never
intended to burn out in any consecrated life.  Physical energy
may burn out, but the fire of God's Spirit in a Christian re-
juvenates even physical senility and enables a well spent Christian life to go out in a blaze of spiritual glory.

The fire of Jesus Christ is kindled in human hearts by the
power of Christ's sacrifice.  It is maintained by the oil of
Divine grace which the believer is encouraged to secure by ever

renewed consecration through the means appointed. A Christian with due awareness of the significance of the fire of Jesus Christ will give priority to every technique by which the volume of that holy fire is spread over every region of human life. No more fundamental service can be rendered by any Christian than to keep life warm in the holy fire of his redemption through Christ so that he will live redemptively with perpetual testimony and unceasing aim to get other lives within the sweep of the fire of Christ.

The fire of Jesus Christ is the world's only hope. Every Christian must keep talking, singing and living in harmony with the lines of the hymn, "Redeeming love has been my theme, and shall be till I die." The world is dying for want of the secret of its redemption. All Christians are men of the secret. What else is there to think or talk about than the holy and redeeming love in the heart of God fully and omnipotently expressed in Christ's death for sin on the Cross? It is the only fire that can stop the world's evil and transmute sinners into servants of the self-giving God and the self-sacrificing Saviour. Keep the heart-fires of experienced grace burning. Keep the mind on Christ and His redemption. Crave ever more of the fire of Jesus Christ. Spread it by lip and life. To get a world without war requires the destruction by the fire of Christ's sacrifice of all the fears, hates, greeds and lusts which produce war. The devil of selfishness must go up in flames.

Study to know what the fire of Jesus Christ has already done for the world. You will learn that there is no other cure for the pagan and demonic than God's sovereign grace in Christ. Never forget the Cross of Christ. Be of those who sing and mean it, "In the Cross of Christ I glory, Towering o'er the wrecks of time. All the light of sacred story, Gathers round that head sublime." May every Christian share Christ's intense desire to have the fire of His loving sacrifice for sin kindled in every human life and work to make desire concrete.

# XVIII

# A Thematic Topical Sermon — Special Form

## Christian Certainties

*By faith we understand.* —HEBREWS 11:3

ALL Christians are spiritual millionaires and sitting on top of the world, if only they knew it. They are not excused from hardship and suffering but resources are theirs to ride on top of all circumstances and to live victoriously and radiantly, no matter what happens. The universe is on the side of all such as have made their peace with God by faith in Jesus Christ. "The trusting heart goes singing."

Christianity ministers to "minds diseased" and has intellectual bread for the questioning spirit. This is indicated by the Scripture verse found in Hebrews eleven, verse three, "By faith we understand that the worlds have been framed by the word of God, so that what is seen hath not been made out of things which appear." This verse treats of the doctrine of creation and is addressed to the question of origin which is of interest to everybody. The mystery of existence has lured the eager mind of man in all ages. It is not our purpose now to discuss the answer given in the Scripture quoted to the problem of beginnings but to unfold the principle contained in the first four words, "By faith we understand." Faith is here said to be a way of knowing, a highway to understanding, a principle of comprehension. The necessity of faith in God's self-revelation is clearly implied. The significance, meaning, nature, character of faith as a technique of Christian certainty is definitely taught. The result of faith is specifically illustrated. Whatever a Christian knows concerning the things that really and eternally matter, he knows because of his faith.

The words of our text, "By faith we understand" suggest the rewards or compensations of Christian faith. The result of being a true believer of all that God has revealed is assurance of all matters necessary to a great life and a great future. A Christian may come to assured and realized possession of certainties. By faith we understand, we get to know, we become sure, we feel certain, we feel the force of, a number of vital facts which make up the content of what we call salvation. The familiar words of the Psalmist declare, "Thou preparest a table before me in the presence of mine enemies." An extension of the meaning of that is lawful. God does just that when he "crowns" the mental table of a Christian with glorious certainties of faith right in the midst of an unbelieving, possibly sneering and contemptuous, world. The festal table of Christian certainties is laden with God's bounteous provision for perpetual daylight and Christians are summoned to take stock and partake. "By faith we understand." Everyone can express the theme in his own way. It is this: Christian faith is the key to Christian knowledge. Questions are natural and pertinent: 1. What does a Christian know? 2. How did he come to know it? Consider, the certainties of the Christian faith; and, secondly, the Secret of Being Sure.

First, the certainties of the Christian faith. Take certain typical certainties. First, the Certainty of the Incarnation of the Son of God. In First John 5:20 we read, "And we know that the Son of God is come, and hath given us an understanding, that we may know him that is true, and we are in him that is true, even in his Son Jesus Christ." The relevant words just now are, "We know that the Son of God is come." We know that God has become man. We know that God has come into our human lot by the gateway of a Divine-human birth. Rightly considered, it is a truth of inconceivable consolation and inspiration that God has not left us to our poor human estate. Once in the long story of human sin, sorrow and struggle, a child was born, concerning whom it could be said,

"This is Immanuel, God with us." O, the wonder and significance of it that the eternal Son of God became man for us men and for our salvation!

Jesus of Nazareth was God in human form. One of the great books of the generation just passed bore the title, *Reality*. The famous theologian who wrote it, put into it the results of thirty years of intellectual toil and struggle. He was a man who had to have a reason for his faith and so he had to fight for it. All his life he fought with intellectual barriers and achieved a reasoned and chastened faith. In discussing the incarnation of the Son of God, he pointed out that personality is the highest we know. How reasonable, creditable, Divinely natural and imperative it was, God being what He is, that God's final and complete self-revelation should be in terms of the highest we know, in terms of a human personality. It was just like God to do this for man, to become man and by so doing bring to full expression His saving will for mankind. A Christian is sure that "the Son of God is come." No wonder an angel heralded the birth, "Be not afraid; for behold, I bring you good tidings of great joy which shall be to all the people: for there is born to you this day in the city of David a Saviour, who is Christ the Lord." A Christian knows that God's promise to visit His people was fulfilled in Jesus the Christ. He is as sure of that as he is of anything. It is a fundamental Christian certainty.

Consider secondly, the certainty of personal salvation. In First John 3:14 we read, "We know that we have passed out of death into life, because we love the brethren." A Christian can be sure he is saved. A Christian knows he has "passed from death into life," that as a Christian he lives in a new world, that old things have passed away, because all things have become new. Before he was a Christian, he may have been either friendly or indifferent or hostile to Christians. Now he knows them for what they are, redeemed souls in Christ Jesus. When he hears a testimony, his heart is strangely warmed. He loves to be where God's people are. He feels a deep concern for all who are in Christ. He suffers in what they suffer. He is ready to do for fellow-Christians what is possible and necessary for their comfort. Once he could think only of self and of those of his own circle in whom self found an avenue of expression and satisfaction. Now he has a new cordiality for fellow-members of the household of faith. He will give and pray and labor for the salvation of all, but God's redeemed people are the objects of Christian love and concern. This is from God. It is Christ who has made the difference. He knows from this that he has passed from death into life, that an old world has been exchanged for a new. "If any man is in Christ, he is a new creature." He is a ransomed soul, a saved man. Every Christian has a right to be sure of his salvation.

Personal salvation is life's most wonderful experience. It surpasses the greatest delights of sensuous enjoyment. It represents the highest, the deepest and the utmost of which human nature is capable. But at that, it is only possible by the miracle of God's saving grace in Christ. No one is unaware of the pleasures of life when he experiences them. Every one has the ordinary satisfactions of normal human beings, the joy of living and being alive, the delight of having good health, agreeable environment and congenial task, and all the pleasures such as of friends, books, travel, music, art and activities which grace average days. Is it not incredible that one should be regenerated by the Holy Spirit of God and not know it? Is it not inconceivable that one has new life in Christ and is unaware of it? If all the delights of mortal existence come as conscious experience, why should the supreme experience of human nature be without identification or conscious rapture? The joy of salvation, the blessedness of it, the awareness of it, goes with salvation. New Testament Christians knew they were saved, knew that they had a new life-center in Christ and that as a consequence, they had passed out of death into life. "I know whom I have believed," said Paul, "and am persuaded that He is able to keep that which I have committed unto Him against that Day." Individual salvation attested by its social expression in love of the brethren, is a certainty of Christian faith.

A third Christian certainty is the Disciplinary Character of Human Life on Earth. "For we know that the whole creation groaneth and travaileth in pain together until now." Romans 8:22. Mankind is part of a process designed to bring creation to a destined goal. "For the earnest expectation of the creation waiteth for the revealing of the sons of God." The best is yet to be. Mortal existence is subject to a law or principle of hope. Nothing here is final. Things are not what they seem. The production of a human race for purposes of eternal glory is big business. Sparks fly when the smith is pounding on the tool he is fashioning or when the potter has a vessel on the grindstone. The present creation is like the vessel marred and being held with sovereign might to Divine purpose of final splendor. A new creation is in the making. Life mortal is the marred vessel in the hand of omnipotent grace. God will make of a fallen race what it pleases Him to make of it and what the intractability of the human clay warrants when God has hold of it.

This third certainty of Christian faith has an obverse side when the apostle Paul says in Romans 8:28, "And we know that all things work together for good to them that love God, to them who are the called according to His purpose." God makes the totality of human experience contributory to the high ends of His grace and glory. Much happens that is utterly bad for everybody, but when it happens to Christians, God so rules and over-rules that the total result of everything combined is for a Christian's eternal good.

God sees to it that everything that happens to a Christian is made to pay toll to his fundamental welfare. God makes the individual calamity part of a system and the system is constructed to benefit Christian believers. The whole universe is under law and constraint to further the spiritual interests of mankind. A Christian is, so to say, never hit by a stray bullet. If he gets hit, God has that bullet in the circle of His design. Beneficent intention controls calamity.

A Christian knows that there is this light of God's all-embracing love on the dark side of life. A status quo of measurable or even marvelous material well-being is not equal to beings made in God's image nor worthy of the structure of human personality. We are in the making. God has something immense in mind. God's super-abounding grace is more than a match for sin and the sinister. A fiery furnace may blaze away at a Christian. He may be tossed right into the fire. But it is the Refiner's fire and the Refiner is God. All a Christian stands to lose is the dross. What he stands to gain is refined gold. Whatever hinders is doomed. Whatever hurts is strictly controlled. Whatever helps, heals, holds, and hoists has atomic force behind it and in it.

A Christian knows the disciplinary character of earthly life. He knows also that all things work together for good to those who know they have passed from death into life. The Son of God is come. Christ is the world's best bet. Christ is man's big chance. To be in Christ is to be in a realm of life where no one can lose. No matter what happens to a Christian, he lives on certainties: the certainty of the Saviour-hood and sovereignty of Jesus Christ, the certainty that while you may be down, you are never out, the certainty that God makes everything you have to bear contribute to your everlasting welfare. A Christian is sure of all this and more.

A fourth Christian certainty is the eternal destiny of a Christian. It has varied expression. Here is one expression, the expression of a Christian's consciousness of the Love Everlasting. "For I am persuaded that neither life nor death . . . shall separate us from the love of God which is in Christ Jesus." Romans 8, verse 38. It is a Christian's destiny to see and be like Jesus Christ. First John 3:2 puts it thus: "Beloved, now are we the sons of God, and it doth not yet appear what we shall be: but we know that when he shall appear, we shall be like him; for we shall see him as he is." In Second Corinthians five, verse one, it is put as the certainty of an eternal, a heavenly home, "For we know that if our earthly house of this tabernacle be dissolved, we have a building from God, an house not made with hands, eternal in the heavens." Personal assurance of a future of everlasting blessedness rests on Christ's assurance to His followers, "I give unto them eternal life and they shall never perish, and no one shall pluck them out of my hand." What a wealth of Christian knowledge is available as the source of assurance, delight and inspiration. We know that we are destined to see and be with and be like Christ. We know that if the worst happens, if death strikes us down, we have an eternal home in heaven. We can be sure of all this. The price of our security has been paid. It is "in the bag," as it were. The Christian life is not an "if" or a "perhaps" or a "maybe" or an "I hope so." It is a case of "we know," "we know," "we know." Christian hope is anchored, not in a fool's Paradise, but within the veil, in the sovereign grace of our risen and ascended Saviour, the Lord and King of life and glory.

A fifth Christian certainty is that God answers Christian prayer. In First John 5, verses 14 and 15, this is affirmed, "And this is the confidence that we have in him, that if we ask anything according to his will he heareth us: And if we know that he hears us, whatsoever we ask, we know that we have the petitions that we desired of him." Prayer according to the will of God is guaranteed an answer, granting the petition. When Christian parents pray for the salvation of a son or daughter, they have every reason to believe that such a prayer will be answered. The answer may not come as soon as expected or asked, because much is involved, including such factors as freedom of choice and the lure of the world, but if such prayer is persisted in and God's leadings are followed, parents who thus pray, can be so sure of an answer that the language is justified when by faith they say, "We know that we have the petitions we desired of him." George Müller of Bristol built and maintained orphanages with prayer and carried them on in utter dependence on God. There were times when of an evening no breakfast was in sight for the children, but always God kept somebody from sleep until the need had been met. Needless to say, this man so mighty in prayer had a deep passion for souls and prayed many a sinner into the kingdom. But there were two men for whose salvation Müller prayed for forty years. They were still unsaved when the man of prayer died, but they were converted after Müller's death. No one looks to God in vain for what God wants every man to have.

The certainties of Christian faith cover not only a Christian's eternal needs, insuring a destiny of final victory over all the dreadful realities of earthly existence, but also his needs in this mortal present, guaranteeing answers to prayer which insure conquering grace here and now.  God is committed even to the temporal care of His people and His people can certainly tell of marvelous Providential deliverances and pro-- visions.  It will seem sometimes to some particular Christian as if God had nothing to do but to take care of him only, so specific, impressive and detailed is God's care of His redeemed people.  It is a most wonderful experience to live in the reali- zation of God's constant care, to be aware that underneath are the everlasting arms, to feel the might of Christ's holding hand.  When real Christians get together socially and open up on God's goodness to them in daily life, it would take a Hallelujah chorus to give a proper finale to the experience meeting.

We know that the Son of God is come, that we have a Divine Saviour Who entered our human lot to redeem, Who illustrated in His human life God's ideal of a man and who laid down His sinless life in order to release and set in motion the power of salvation.  We know that we have passed from death into life, that we are Christians, that Christ has actually, really and truly saved us, giving us new world for old.  We know that the Christian life, like human life generally, is dis- ciplinary, that hard things have to be borne, but that God is with us and in our experiences to make all of them, even the most terrible, work in conjunction with total life-experiences for a Christian's eternal benefit.  We know that we shall live forever and be forever with Christ and become like Him, and have suitable habitation for our redeemed human personalities. We know that God answers prayer when we live in His will, with ears open to every cry and resources at His command to give us daily, hourly victory. Every Christian has it in him to repeat with Deuteronomy 29, verse 29, "The secret things belong unto the Lord our God; but those things which are revealed belong unto us and our children." Remember, too, what Paul says in I Cor. 2:9,10,11,12: "Things which eye saw not, and ear heard not God prepared for them that love him. But unto us God revealed them through the Spirit: for the Spirit searcheth all things, yea, the deep things of God." Thus is set forth the great field of Christian certainty and the festal table is all set, as it were, for a spiritual banquet.

The question now remains. How is a Christian made sure? How can any person possess as his own personal realized possession these Christian certainties? How does one get in on all this? Consider, "the Christian's Secret of Being Sure." Hebrews 11:6 says, "And without faith it is impossible to be well-pleasing unto him," that is, well-pleasing unto God, "for he that cometh to God must believe that he is, and that he is a rewarder of them that seek after him." It is necessary to believe God, to accept Jesus Christ in all the value of his self-revelation, to take God's Word for things, to go by what God says, to trust God absolutely, to stake your all for time and for eternity on Christ, to bet your life on Him.

The universe is so constructed that man has to look to God for things. The way of things is such that man is a dependent creature. He comes to his own only by giving up his self-will. He may think and feel that he is monarch of all he surveys but his ownership of anything is at long last only a short-term lease. He may shout, "I am the captain of my soul; I am the master of my fate." True enough, but he will surely prove a captain who goes down with his ship, unless he takes Christ as his pilot. And the fate of which he is master is eternal destruction from the presence of the Lord unless he puts his case in the hands of the eternal, sovereign Christ who alone can save him. Man has lost his way and his own ways are all detours which run dead and lead to frustration and disintegration. Man cannot make a go of it all by himself. The universe is too big. Life is a trackless wilderness to those who are blind to God. Human self-sufficiency is no match for infinite issues and eternal destiny. Man needs God. He needs Christ Whom God sent to be the Saviour of the world. "Who is the liar but he that denieth that Jesus is the Christ?" Liars have no future in a universe built on and for truth. Faith in Christ is the fundamental necessity.

Faith in Christ and in God's full self-revelation is not only a fundamental necessity but ranks first among spiritual priorities. You start with faith. To believe is the initial response to God's overtures of Grace. Proof comes after faith and is given only to those who believe. God does not certify Himself to unbelievers except as judge of their wickedness. Unbelief is the basic sin, source of all other sin and sins.

If one demands proof before he believes, he will never know anything. Such an attitude may get by in a world where all men are liars according to the hasty judgment of the Psalmist, but it gets no one anywhere with God. It is the Supreme Moral Being of the universe with Whom man has to do. God has laid it down that faith is the starting-point to anywhere and everywhere with Him. Whoever wants to go places and see and do things in realms of true life and light, in spheres of Christian certainties and answered prayers, in the vast Homeland of the soul, believes first and then travels. Faith is your ticket to board the train. You lay in dust life's glory dead and give Christ your soul, your life, your all. That puts you "all-aboard" with bag and baggage left behind because God furnishes everything in Christ. Everything is planned, arranged, provided, taken care of, guaranteed. You stake all to gain all. A person has to come to it to make a clean breast of everything, to make a full surrender, not insisting on retention of prerogatives, letting go of anything and everything in the way of pseudo-divine emperors or spurious divine rights. A man can perish even in the sea of God's grace unless he quits fighting the waves and relaxes and trusts himself to the waters of God's redemption. Fight them and down you go. Trust them, let yourself go, and they hold you up and waft you safe on Heaven's happy shore.

What a salvation God has in store for floundering and frustrated intellectuals if only they take their brains with their self-will and throw all into the lap of Christ! All who think they know better than God had better sign on the dotted line for Christ. Only faith, Christian faith, faith in the testimony of God, faith in Christ will save any and all. The moment one puts it all up to Christ and himself at Christ's disposal, he sets his foot on a vast unexplored continent of Christian truth and certainties. The splendor of the Christian life is its exploration of the wealth of this domain which God crowns with progressive discovery of the things freely given. Believe and live. Believe and know. Believe and be sure. "By faith we understand."

Meanwhile, Christians have reason to sing the hymn, "My Father is rich" and to repeat the chorus, "I'm the child of a King, the child of a King. With Jesus my Saviour, I'm the child of a King."

# XIX

# A Thematic Textual Sermon

## Christ and World Crisis

*Now is the judgment of this world; now shall the prince of this world be cast out.* —JOHN 12:31

THESE words of our Lord furnish a key to the meaning of history. That Jesus was able to make such a statement when the world was about to crucify Him sets Him apart as the one infallible interpreter of history. What current events seem to say is one thing; what is really said and done by what is happening is quite another. The verdict of current events is never final except in so far as it squares with Divine purpose and ultimate reality. Other current events and further historical happenings are in prospect which will judge the achievements of iniquity.

At the time Jesus made the statement under consideration, it was He who apparently was on the spot. It was He Who faced condemnation, judgment, and doom. The authorities were in the seat of the mighty. Everything seemed to be very much in their hands. They thought everything would be as they decreed. It might be expected that Jesus would share their views and that he would say what anyone whom they considered a deluded enthusiast would say under similar circumstances. Little did they realize that Jesus was not victim but victor, that his present situation had been foreseen and brought about by Himself in pursuit of His saving mission as the incarnate Son of God. While the authorities acted in the full exercise of moral freedom, Jesus was doing the same. He had steadfastly set His face toward fulfilling complete self-giving. Here was a set of circumstances in which man was doing his very worst and God was doing His very best, as Dan Crawford, noted missionary, once expressed it.

"Now is the judgment of this world; now the prince of this world shall be cast out." In these words Jesus gives us His understanding of what was going on. He turns the tables on those who plan to be rid of Him. They are conscious of being judges of Jesus, but Jesus makes the point that what they propose to do to Him is a judgment on themselves. They represent the world in their animosity and therefore the essential spirit of the world is involved in what is done to Jesus. The term "crisis" has also been used to render the Greek word translated "judgment" and a footnote in the margin of the Bible puts the indefinite article before it. "Now is a crisis of this world. Now is a judgment of this world. Now the prince of this world shall be cast out."

It has been said that the history of the world is the judgment of the world. The state of the world is the result of the behaviour of the world. What happens in the world is a key to human character and the harvest of man's deeds. The world is thus always in a state of crisis and the work of judgment goes on unceasingly. But crucial as all the times are and continuous as judgment is on all that man does, there are times which are specially critical, times when the evil in men and institutions has a sort of full and final expression, times when events register judgment with an unusual degree of finality on some sinister spirit and action of man.

The continuous process of judgment which is operative in history may be thought of as a series of judgments. One judgment in the series was unalterably fixed by the world's condemnation and crucifixion of Jesus. The condemnation and crucifixion of Jesus brought crisis and judgment to the generation then living. The fact that one like Jesus was crucified constitutes the condemnation of the world. It can always be said against the world that it crucified Jesus. What happened to the generation of Jesus' day was brought on by what the generation of Jesus' day did to Jesus.

What happens to the world in any generation is brought on by what any generation does about Jesus Christ. The way the world treats Christ settles human prospects. Rejection of Christ is progressively ruinous and ultimately fatal. When those who cried, "Crucify him, crucify him," had their way with respect to Jesus, the crisis for them was on and their doom was sealed. The answer the world gives to Christ is of critical importance. Rejection of Christ inaugurates crisis. Always the supreme question is, "What think ye of Christ?" Human society, as organized apart from Christ, brings pressure to bear against Christ. Just as the pressure on a submarine increases in proportion to its depth, so pressure against Christ increases according to the degree of personal immersion in the life of the world. "What concord has Christ with Belial?" The pressure becomes intolerable and the Pilate in every one asks, "What then shall I do with Jesus?" Everything depends on the soul's response to that question.

The world shouts, "Let him be crucified." If that voice carries the day, it means the blackout of the light by which man lives. Decision against Christ is crisis pregnant with judgment and doom. Here, surely, "whatsoever a man sows, that shall he reap." Relationship to Christ in the long run determines the state of the world. It determines personal character and destiny.

The world is in the grip of a terrific crisis, a crisis brought on by the responsible action of self-willed behaviour, which, therefore, makes the crisis a judgment of God on man's determined rebellion against the sovereign Christ. And because Christ is sovereign, He will win all wars. The incarnate wickedness arrayed against Him will be cast out. Critical issues are in the balance from day to day. But the kingdom of God is at stake, that kingdom which an archbishop of Canterbury defined as "love endowed with power and power subordinate to love." The kingdom of God is destined to overcome and absorb all earthly kingdoms. At present the most diabolical hate is rampant, hate endowed with immense power and power the implement of hate. Hate will have its day, but love is here to stay, the love of God in Christ which redeems and saves.

"Only the stars are neutral" says the title of a book. That title is untrue. "The stars in their courses fought against Sisera" and they fight against all embodied wickedness and hate. The stars are a part of the structure of the universe and the universe is constructed on the principle of self-giving love. True love is righteous and pure. True love is merciful. True love is sacrificial. Such love is the essence of God's eternal life. Such love, incarnate in Jesus Christ, the Son of God and the world's Redeemer, is indestructible and sovereign. At the root of the universe this eternal, all-conquering love is found. The stars are not neutral. The universe is not neutral. The stars and the universe are on the side of Christ, of righteousness, of love and of true humanity.

The course of our meditation is clear. First, the crisis of our age; second, the crisis of our age as a judgment on the world; third, the sure victory of the kingdom of God, of the conquering Christ, of those who fight to preserve and increase the fruit of Christ's sacrifice in the earth.

Consider, then, the crisis of our age. A professor of sociology at Harvard University devotes a book to the crisis of our age. Here is one picture he gives, "We are in the midst of an enormous conflagration burning everything into ashes. In a few weeks millions of human lives are uprooted; in a few hours century-old cities are demolished; in a few days kingdoms are erased. Red human blood flows in broad streams from one end of the earth to the other. Ever-expanding misery spreads its gloomy shadow over larger and larger areas. The fortunes, happiness and comfort of untold millions have disappeared. Peace, security and safety have vanished. Prosperity and well-being have become in many countries but a memory; freedom a myth. Western culture is covered by a blackout. A great tornado sweeps over the whole of mankind." These few sentences suggest the appalling realities which symbolize the crisis of our age.

The Harvard sociologist gives a comprehensive diagnosis of the state of the world. Indeed, his diagnosis takes in the past as well as the present. Centuries of history are brought under the microscope of searching investigation. Dr. Sorokin believes that the life of mankind, in all its varied expressions, is determined by its dominant culture. Human beings live the way they think. "Out of the heart are the issues of life." "As a man thinketh, so he is." If enough people think a certain way, the life ensuing will express that way of thought. The arts and sciences will express it. Philosophy and religion will feel its impact, as also law and ethics. Social, economic and political organization will register the prevailing convictions. Dr. Sorokin takes up the various compartments of world-life and shows how for four hundred years now, the major principle of European and American culture has been this-worldly, secular, utilitarian, sensory, sensate. "Only what we see, hear, smell, touch, and otherwise perceive through our sense organs is real and has value."

Our modern world has been fully committed to exploring the possibilities of life in terms of the physical, the sensuous and the material. Science has made giant strides in multiplying the means of giving people a good time. One of the leading industries of America is the motion-picture industry, an instrument of pleasure for untold millions. Think of the realms of food, of drink, of dress, of housing, of travel, of entertainment, of business and commerce, of education and social life, and one is soon overwhelmed by the vast expenditure of human resources to minister to humanity on the side of the physical and material. Even religion has been harnessed to secular objects as a means of holding the dwindling allegiance of decreasing congregations. If the spires of church steeples symbolize man's aspiration Godward, the institutional church bears witness to the preeminence of social ministry over wide areas of church life. There can be little doubt that many people attend church with the sense of doing somebody a favor. If attendance is to continue they must have assurance that they will *enjoy* the sermon and the music. Such a practice is like expecting a doctor to diagnose a case as per order and indicates at any rate that secular idealism is dominant also in religious circles. The only reason for a church service is the public worship of God, the exposure of life to revealed truth and the grateful reception of God's redeeming grace in Christ.

When it is said that the dominant culture is secular, utilitarian and sensory, there is no preconceived intention of being censorious or casting aspersions on the human. Life in the body has its needs, its rights and its claims. There are large ranges of the lawful and the lovely in the physical life of mankind. We stress now the world's sense of the importance of the sensory and secular. The modern world is for one world at a time. It is for this present world. It has spent treasures of mentality and energy with immense ingenuity to cram life full to overflowing with human interest and pleasure.

One may ask, "What has this to do with the crisis of our age?" Just this. Dr. Sorokin points out that our sensate culture does more than say that the true reality and value is sensory. Quoting Dr. Sorokin, "Beyond such a sensory reality, either there is nothing, or if there is something, we cannot sense it; therefore it is equivalent to the non-real and the non-existent." Imagine that! According to sensate culture there is no God or if there is, you cannot sense Him and therefore God is equivalent to the non-real and the non-existent. There you have the real heart of modern culture. This virtually atheistic viewpoint has been in the seat of the mighty for a long time. It has carried the day on the practical issues of life. Its voice has been the voice of the majority. It has been the controlling force in human society. It has been like a universal contagion, laying a blighting hand on everybody and everything, secularizing the life of the world, blacking-out God, eternity, spirituality, humane spirit and jeopardizing, altering, degrading and destroying the values, institutions and relationships which come out of man's faith in God and man's fellowship with God.

A dominant secular culture means a dominant drift toward Paganism and that is just what the world is suffering from. That is the crisis of our age. It is that which endangers us and which we are fighting. Humanity cannot stay human if it rules God out. A secular culture glorifies life here and now and brings immeasurable expansion and expression to man's craving for pleasure. It may splurge for centuries with unbounded creative force, stealing the liveries of heaven to serve the Devil in, but at long last, its essential godlessness, heartlessness and beastliness will be exposed in a reign of terror one would not naturally believe to be possible. In a day when crooners, concentrated on sensuous enjoyment, steal the language of religion to describe carnal delights and broadcast the preeminence of the sensory in words like "This is heaven" or "Heaven can wait," the ultimate blasphemy is a reality and bad men may be expected to stoop to anything to gain base ends.

Listen now to one further quotation from *The Crisis of Our Age* by Dr. Sorokin: "We are living and acting at one of the epoch-making turning points of human history, when one form of culture and society-sensate — is declining and a different form is emerging. The crisis is also extraordinary in the sense that, like its predecessors, it is marked by an extraordinary explosion of wars, revolutions, anarchy and bloodshed, by social, moral, economic, political, and intellectual chaos; by a resurgence of revolting cruelty and animality, and a temporary destruction of the great and small values of mankind; by misery and suffering on the part of millions — a convulsion far in excess of the chaos and disorganization of the ordinary crises. Such transitional periods have always been the veritable day of wrath, that day."

Such is the crisis of our age. Consider secondly, that this crisis of our age is a judgment of God upon rampant and regnant practical atheism. "Now is *the* judgment of this world" and "now is *a* judgment of this world." The world is always judged by what it does to Jesus Christ, Who is God incarnate and the only rightful King of humanity. A secular age that crucifies Christ afresh digs its own grave with hell on earth preceding. A world that casts its majority vote against Christ votes its own doom. Given enough humans who put self in God's place and all moral imperatives and sanctions are on the way to the scrap heap. The earth becomes a grab-bag and human life a scramble. When the majority vote of mankind is that there is no God, it means every man for himself and the vast ills which such a conviction makes possible. But God does not abdicate because men live as if there is no God. "The wrath of God is revealed from heaven against all unrighteousness of men who hold down the truth of God in unrighteousness." The world today is experiencing a concrete revelation of the wrath of God, of the wrath of the redeeming God. God's judgments are in the earth. The measure of their operation is the measure of man's rebellion and disobedience. In keeping God's commandments there is great reward, but defiance of God, contempt for His honor, indifference to His holiness and scorn for His love call into action the Divine revulsion toward human sin and guilt. The wages of sin is death and the present era is one of those recurring pay-days when God brings humanity to a better mind.

Karl Barth makes an illuminating comment on the wrath of God in his commentary on the Epistle to the Romans. Barth defines the wrath of God as "the righteousness of God without Christ." In Jesus Christ God offers erring humanity His forgiving and regenerating grace. The Christian Gospel is good news from God, the good news of mercy for the sinner and a new creative beginning for all who put their trust in Christ. God in Christ confronts humanity with the offer of pardon and new life. God has, so to speak, taken man's sin into His own heart. The death of Christ on Calvary's cross has such significance that it was true to say, as the apostle Paul did, "God was in Christ reconciling the world unto Himself, not imputing unto men their trespasses." Speaking of Christ, the same apostle said, "Him Who knew no sin, God made to be sin on our behalf that we might become the righteousness of God in Him." God's offer to humanity in Christ is man's one best chance.

The world thus faces two alternatives: Christ and His salvation or the righteousness of God without Christ. It can have forgiveness and redemption through the one only living Saviour or it must experience the righteousness of God without Christ, which means the working out of the moral order of the universe.

It is at this point that the Bible view of man and man's view of himself are fundamentally at variance. The Bible views man as morally and spiritually bankrupt, with liabilities far in excess of assets. Man appraises himself as morally and spiritually solvent. The Bible insists on man's need of a Redeemer and redemption. Man insists on his self-sufficiency to operate his own life and to meet all requirements of the human situation. The Bible proclaims human inability to square life with the demands of a moral world order. Man proceeds as if human resources are entirely adequate. There you have the fundamental breach between God and man.

One does not need to depreciate the good in man or cast aspersions on man's abilities, to demonstrate that the Bible is right. Humanity can build a marvelous civilization but lacks the moral will and purpose to operate it in harmony with the divine idea. Technological progress is registered in unnumbered achievements of human ingenuity and skill, but an evil heart of unbelief rules out a God of love and righteousness and deifies the unregenerate passions of sinful human nature. An age that can justly boast of streamlined progress in the realm of the physical and material lacks the moral resources of brotherly behaviour. Man can do marvelous things, but he cannot control himself, he cannot behave himself, he cannot treat his fellowman as the brother for whom Christ died. He arms himself with power and uses it to smite. He feels no need of a Divine interposition in the interest of deliverance from what's wrong. He wants to be on his own and spurns the gospel of God's forgiving grace in Christ. He turns his back to the offered mercy of the Redeemer and faces the moral order of the universe with an unwarranted sense of solvency.

How can hate win in a world built for love? How can greed finally prosper in an order designed for self-giving? How can humanity flourish when self-will rules the majority? Love, service, obedience, sacrifice, righteousness and power harnessed to benevolent purpose are the key-factors in a healthy human society. An age that sets itself against these in the interest of unbridled egoism has the universe to deal with and is doomed, no matter how great its power or however prolonged its tyranny.

The dominant culture of godless selfishness has come to a crisis, to a judgment of God, to a revelation of the wrath of God against the unrighteousness of men. God's offer of salvation in Christ is rejected by the vast majority. Supernatural interposition is repudiated. Man chooses to go on without the grace of the Saviour. He faces the operative righteousness of God without Christ. Never forget that man is reaping what he has sown, that he is getting what he chose and that the experience of the Divine reaction to the secular idealism and vulgar egoism of a sensory age is freighted with redemptive love and interest.

Consider finally, the assured victory of the cause of God. "Now shall the prince of this world be cast out." People in their confusion about world events ask, "Why does not God do something?" The answer is that God is doing plenty. God is casting out the prince of this world. God is demonstrating that an age which confines reality and value to what the organs of sense certify cannot last. God is showing what it is in the heart of such a sensate, selfish culture to become and perpetrate. When man's natural selfishness is seen illustrated in its ultimate essence and consequence on the gigantic scale afforded by totalitarian despotism, the Divine intention is that men may repent and turn to the only true God our Saviour. The selfishness in one and all at long last produces world tyrants. The sacrificial costliness of overcoming and ridding the earth of such dictators is the Divine technique for purging all hearts and inducing mankind to seek contact with the one solitary source of man's regeneration, our Lord and Saviour Jesus Christ.

God has brought humanity to a halt. God has man stopped. A world that repudiates God and recognizes no Divine purpose in mortal existence forfeits the right to go on. There is no reason why mankind should be allowed the enjoyment of life and the use of earth's resources when everything is increasingly prostituted to carnal uses. When life tends to become ever more and more an orgy of unbridled indulgence, a point is reached where men make up their minds that the only thing to do is to fight and kill one another off. One pairs up with another and presently the earth is an armed camp. Shrewd all-inventing man now marshalls ingenuity and skill to destroy. All human resources are commandeered. Millions are turned away from the usual pursuits of human life to join the hosts of destruction. To such a pass has humanity come. To such a point, self-will brings humanity. It must be clear that God will not stand for a world whose culture regards God as non-real, non-existent or unknowable.

"Now shall the prince of this world be cast out." God has His people also and His armies. Sinful as His people and armies are, He will use them and equip them to stem the tide of incarnate hate and greed and to keep alive and operative the blood-bought gains of His Divine crusade of redemption. Too long has the Devil had his way. The devilishness of the godless has gone too far. The boundaries of the proprieties have been overstepped with flagrant maliciousness. The day of reckoning is on. A new age is in the birth. An epoch has closed. The Son of God will see of the travail of His soul and be satisfied. The price for deliverance from brutal power will be costly, because the evil is universal and deep-seated. Whatever is to be suffered, the price must be paid. God will give ability and grace to pay it.

When Jesus was crucified, the world planned to be done with Christ forever. It amounted to an all-out offensive to kill God and to be rid of Him. To such ruin had man come, man made in God's image, man the crown of God's creation. So in our modern world. Man is by majority disposition through with God. Self-worship is his religion. Self-indulgence is his creed. God is not in all his thoughts.

As sure as God is God, He will not stand for it. He is not standing for it. Our miseries are great upon us in order that we may turn to Christ and be delivered from that soul-destroying monster sin. The mortal crisis is on. The prince of the world is being cast out. The prince of the world recognizes only one reality, physical force. God's arsenal includes that weapon for such as the prince of this world. But the kingdom of God! We build it by faith in Jesus Christ and love of our fellowmen through grace. We fight to arrest the destroyer. We repent and believe the Gospel in order to put on the whole armour of God for the building of His kingdom, the kingdom of "love endowed with power and power subordinate to love."

# XX

# A Thematic Doctrinal Sermon

## Does the Church Matter?

*Now ye are the body of Christ, and severally members thereof.*
— I Cor. 12:27

THE Christian Church is the most important institution on earth. Jesus declared it to be indestructible when He said that the gates of hell should not prevail against it. It belongs to Christ, Who referred to it as "my church," claiming it as exclusively His. It is an organization composed of all such as are true believers in Jesus Christ, the Son of God and Saviour of the world. It embraces all God's redeemed people, the multitude of such as have placed their trust in Christ as personal Saviour and as the Master of their lives. It includes people of every race and nation, of every class of human society, of every age group, with no barrier to entrance except impenitence and unbelief. It removes all reasons for either superiority or inferiority complexes, bringing every believer to his greatest possible significance.

If the Christian Church is so great, so important, so significant, it follows that to be a Christian and a member of the Christian Church is the highest honor any person can have. Membership in the Church of Christ lifts life to a dignity and meaning only possible by an act of God. It pays to go into the matter, to get the right idea about the Church and to weigh the privilege and responsibility of being a Christian, a member of the Christian Church. The heart of the matter is in the text chosen for this sermon, "Now ye are the body of Christ, and severally members thereof." A Christian who exposes himself to the idea that he is a member of the body of Christ will never be in doubt about the meaning and importance of the Christian life. When he informs himself of the circumstances under which the text was written, he will know the solution of all problems which have to do with the relation of Christians to one another. The whole matter can be expressed in the condensed statement, "What the Christian Church is to Christ sets the standard for Christian behaviour." Since the Church is composed of individuals, it will serve to put the word "Christians" in the place of the words "The Christian Church" and to express the theme of this sermon thus: "What Christians are to Christ sets the standard for Christian behaviour." Keeping close to what the apostle Paul says makes it clear that in the church to which he wrote, the members did not get along together as well as might have been expected of a church which had such remarkable spiritual gifts. Paul discusses with inspired wisdom the unity and variety of spiritual gifts, using the idea of the Church as the body of Christ as a proper figure for Christian relations within the Church. He seeks to impress that "what Christians are to Christ shows what they are to one another." Paul's teaching serves to instruct the Christian Church in all ages that "what Christians are to Christ sets the standard for Christian behaviour." What Christians are to Christ suggests the function of the Church in human society and answers the question, "Does the Church matter to the world?" What Christians ought to be to one another suggests the function of the Church in the Church and answers the question, "Does the Church matter to the Church?" To learn the mind of God on these great subjects will suggest the Church's failure to measure up to its function and will answer the question, "What is the matter with the Church?"

Consider, first, the function of the Church in human society. Does the Church matter to the world? The Christian Church is the instrument of Christ's self-expression in the life of the world. What Christians are to Christ is indicated by the figure of the Church as the body of Christ. The body of any person is absolutely necessary to life and activity in this world. No one can qualify as a member of the human race without a body.

The body is the house a person lives in. Without a body, a person is done with this world. The Church as the body of Christ affords residence to Jesus Christ in human society.

Christ as risen and ascended is now in heaven in the body of His glory, His spiritual resurrection body. He is at the right hand of God in the place of power. But at Pentecost He became a living spiritual presence in the hearts of Christian believers, that is to say, in His body, the Church. This is really too wonderful for words. The Christ Who became incarnate, Who suffered and died for the sins of the world, Who arose from the dead and ascended into heaven in the incorruptible body of His risen life, became reincarnate in the Church, in the bodies of Christian believers, dwelling in their hearts through the power of the Holy Spirit.

Once the eternal Son of God became incarnate by the gateway of a Divine-human birth. He was born of the virgin Mary, the only begotten Son of the Father. He did what He did in the days of His flesh, being Immanuel, God with us. At Pentecost He became reincarnate, but this time not in one body specially prepared and provided by God, but in the bodies of Christians, who constitute His Church. Christ became reincarnate in His Church, individual Christians all together constituting His body and being severally, each in appointed part, members of the body of Christ. Christ is no longer a member of human society as he was in the days of His flesh. The removal of the body of His flesh from the earth has not severed His connection with the human race, however. He continues present and active in this world in His body the Church, becoming reincarnate in every "born of God" Christian. Christ has His home in Christian hearts and those in whom He thus lives through their faith in Him and by the power of the Holy Spirit are to reincarnate His Spirit and be thus truly members of the body of Christ. What the body of Jesus meant to Jesus when He was on earth in the days of His flesh, the Church as the body of Christ now means to Christ for the continuance of His presence and saving work on earth while as to visible form He is no longer here.

Christians are the body of Christ, the organism in which His living presence in this world is a reality and an operative power. Whatever Christ means to the world today is registered in the significance to the world of His Church. Whatever Christ is doing now in this present time He is doing through His body the Church. The sovereign Christ from His seat of power in heaven has chosen the Church on earth to be His body, to contain His life and Spirit, to represent Him, to obey His orders, carry on His work and carry out His plans. The significance of Christ to the world today is all up to Christians who are His body, to enshrine His Spirit and be to Him the one only present form of His self-expression on earth.

Does the Christian Church matter to the world? Without the Christian Church, this would be a Christless world, a world without a Saviour, a world lost in the darkness of sin, a world without Christian ideals or Christian conscience. Bad as the world is, untold good wrought by Christ in and through His body the Church, constitutes that higher life of the world which is the effective curb of atomic brutality. Christian idealism draws strength and sustenance from the idea of the Church as the body of Christ. Christians are thrilled and inspired to every good word and work by the sense that they have this supreme value to Christ as the organism of His functioning in the field of mankind's natural depravity. The object of all Christian life and activity is to represent Christ. A real Christian discounts personal likes and dislikes. The ideal Christian motive is not personal self-expression, but to qualify as a channel of Christ's self-expression. As members of the body of Christ, Christians are aware that their lives must be all and only for and through Jesus Christ.

It is impressive beyond words that Christ has by His own action no other medium of action on earth than the lives of Christians who constitute His body the Church. This new and better world which we feel must be built to save civilization from destroying itself can only be built on one foundation and that foundation is Christ. Only Christ can really build the better world that is to be and must be. But Christ uses His body the Church to do in the world and for the world all that it is in His heart to do. Christ has what it takes to bring in world salvation but His body the Church must act in all areas in complete harmony with His mind and pay the cost at every point and at all times of serving as Christ's body only. It is gallant to sing, "Christ for the world we sing. The world to Christ we bring, with loving zeal." To do what we sing requires the last full measure of devotion from every Christian. Again and again a Christian must examine himself with the question, "What kind of a church would my church be if every Christian were just like me?"

Christ gives to every Christian the matchless priority of representing Him in this world. To every saved soul is given the dignity, the honor, the value of being a member of His body the Church. This means that Christ makes His home in the heart. The living presence of Christ in the heart assures an up-to-date salvation, the rapture of pardon, the gladness of peace, the joy of life in Christ, sense of purpose, experienced power for the high ends of Christ's glory, progressive victory over temptation, triumph over circumstances, sense of true well-being, the far horizons of the soul, effective witness to grace received and Christ's use of life for saving the lost and building the kingdom of God. The Church as the body of Christ need fear no depressions, no unemployment, no frustration, no disintegration, no futile Christlike endeavors. Christ is the life and the prize of His people, insuring perpetual solvency under all circumstances, giving and being always all sufficiency for all things.

Does all this matter to the world? Does the Church matter to the world? As surely as Christ is the hope of the world, so surely does the Church which is Christ's body matter to the world. The Church is Christ visible and effective in human society. The Church is the formal and dynamic proof of Christ's competence. The Church is Christ seeking to save. The Church is a living organism, animated by the Spirit of Christ, possessing His mind, affording residence to His significance for modern man and modern life. The Church is foretoken, prophecy and first-fruits of Christ's redeeming grace. Christians are living epistles of Christ's magnificence. The Church is revelation and demonstration of man's restoration in Christ. The world has never seen the like of an organization with as many members in allotted place and filling allotted part as the Christian Church. The Jesus of Nazareth has become the Christ of the nations and the Saviour of the world functioning through His self-chosen body, the Church. The Christian Church is Christ spreading Himself out in visible vital form all over the earth, all through the centuries, through all areas of human life and need to approve Himself as the qualified Redeemer and making Himself available to a stricken world. The Church is Christ proving Himself indispensable, inescapable, endlessly resourceful, the universal lover and benefactor of fallen humanity. The Church is Christ the great Physician ministering the regenerating, healing, cleansing and vitalizing therapy of Christ's power to save to a world in sore straits. Christ sets great store by His people, honors them, makes them partners in His work, channels of His power, agents of His love, instruments of His salvation, ambassadors of good-will, functioning as body to His eternal Spirit. Christians need a deeper sense of the honor Christ confers in order that they may awaken to a sense of their privilege and responsibility.

The fact that Christians are members of the body of Christ sets the standard for Christian behaviour. If the Church as the body of Christ matters supremely to the world, does the Church matter to those who are in it? Consider the standard of Christian behaviour suggested by the conception of the Church as the body of Christ. If Christians are severally members of the body of Christ, they are necessary and vital to one another. They are mutually interdependent. If one suffers, all suffer. If one functions as it should, all are served. There can be no occasion for jealousy, rivalry, preeminence or inferiority. The situation calls for unity, fellowship, brotherhood, cooperation, mutual respect, social service. What a

Christian is to Christ must settle once and for all how he regards and behaves toward his brethren in Christ.

In the world special gifts single people out as entitled to special honor. Human society develops and exhibits classifications of people and one is fundamentally regarded as of more significance than others. Humanity is not naturally a brotherhood, human nature being what it is. Yet ideally that is just what humanity should be. Four-fifths of the world's work must be pure drudgery. The work is there and must be done if humanity is to survive. Those who do the drudgery have not been duly regarded and rewarded. They have all too often had to fight for their rights. The constant strife which marks the life of mankind is due to "man's inhumanity to man," his lack of brotherliness, his greed for gold and lust for power, contempt for fellowmen, arrogant insistence on being some great one entitled to sit on top of the world and lord it over others. It was never God's idea that the world should be a grab-bag and that all men should be go-getters with the motto, "First come, first served." It is God's idea that the human race should be a brotherhood with each serving the welfare of all and all rejoicing in the mutual service of each. Nature is at our service. God is at our service. Christ is at our service. The structure of the universe and the totality of its forces are all at humanity's service. How then can it go well with man and be well on earth when man rebels against the way of things and decides to get his, no matter what? It just is not in the nature of things for man to prosper unless he gets under the load of the burden of life to do his part to lift everybody up and help everybody out. Brotherhood, God's Fatherhood, the conception of humanity as a family, mutual love and service are written into the structure of the universe and constitute the fundamental law of the kingdom of God.

Mankind being what it is, God undertook to carry out His original idea anyhow. He sent His Son to be the second Adam, the Head of a new humanity. Christ came to redeem the world, to make atonement for sin, to communicate God's own true Divine life to those who would put their trust in Him.

So it is that Paul declares, "If any man is in Christ he is a new creature," a new creation. The new body of believers in Christ becomes the Christian Church upon which Christ confers the unspeakable honor of constituting His body on earth, the home of His Spirit, His means of carrying on in a world that has missed it and lost out. Every individual Christian is endowed with membership in this body of Christ. It is evident that the Church of Christ is thus the new humanity already created by regeneration through the Holy Spirit but also in process of construction and development as a perfect medium of Christ's self-expression. Man's moral freedom carries over into the Christian life but the resources are available for redeemed sinners to function in unity as members of the body of Christ.

Christians can only be to one another what they ought to be by constantly keeping it before them what they are to Christ and that therefore their possibilities in Christ constitute their Christian responsibility. Disposition and action toward fellow Christians are to be channels of Christ's self-expression. It is not what self wants and dictates which is to regulate Christian relations toward fellow Christians, but what Christ wants and inspires. The famous book, *In His Steps,* portrayed results of Christians' shaping conduct by the question, "What would Jesus do?" But even that does not go far enough for Christians who are members of the body of Christ. Paul's statement, "Christ liveth in me" is nearer to the heart of the matter. As a member of the body of Christ, a Christian is really Christ functioning through him. Self is only a channel. A member of a body responds to the central control, to the spirit animating the body. So a Christian prays, "Use me Lord. Work through me. Make me a channel, Lord. Make me responsive to Thy will. May what I do be Christ at work through me."

Christians are the body of Christ. Each individual Christian is a member of the body of Christ. What does this mean? It signifies unity of origin, variety of function and equality of

value. Look at these matters in turn. There is an inherent
unity among Christians. We have named it unity of origin.
Every one who is a Christian is a Christian because he is
saved by grace. Every Christian owes his salvation, his Christian life and prospects to an act of God, God's action in Christ.
Paul makes it clear that all boasting is excluded. If any one
wants to glory, let him glory in the Lord. No Christian has
anything in himself to brag about. "What hast thou that thou
has not received and why shouldest thou glory as if Thou hadst
not received it." "Of God are ye in Christ Jesus" says Paul.
Nothing is clearer than that man can not save himself. His
moral progress lags far behind his material advance. If one is
a Christian he can but sing, "O the love that sought me! O
the blood that bought me! O the grace that brought me to the
fold! Wondrous grace that brought me to the fold!" There is
no place in the rapture of pardon and in the joy of salvation
either for a superiority complex or an inferiority complex. A
superiority complex underrates Christ and overrates self. An
inferiority complex likewise underrates Christ, implying that
when Jesus saves, nothing was saved that matters. A Christian
is never a nobody. He is a member of the body of Christ and
because of his spiritual origin in being born again, in being
born of God by regeneration of the Holy Spirit and his incorporation into the body of Christ, he is entitled to respect
himself of what he is to Christ and what Christ makes him to
his fellow Christians as a member of His body. Unity of
origin implies unity of life, of spirit, of faith, of confession,
of possession, of sustenance, of inspiration, of privilege, of
responsibility, of relationship to Christ, of atmosphere, of
environment, of security, of prestige, of suffering, of hope,
of love, of destiny. To be members of Christ's body is to be
one in Christ and the total meaning of that is enough for
perfect peace.

Since Christians are severally members of the body of Christ,
variety of function is indicated. The field of human personality
exhibits endless variety. Psychology may put them into a few

outstanding types, but circumstances and reactions thereto are numerous enough to run into large figures. In human society as organized apart from Jesus Christ, every person has an allotted place and part determined by ability or necessity or preference. Sinful though mankind is, cooperation is imperative in civilization and the world's life is thus seen to be in measure a cooperative enterprise. But in the Christian Church, the Divine ideal of fraternal relations is to have its perfect expression. All Christians have the Holy Spirit as their common possession, but there are also special endowments conferred upon specific individuals so that the life of the Christian Church may reach the highest levels of spiritual well-being and Christian enthusiasm. Christ is not the Dispenser of a drab monotony. No one Christian has everything. Not a single Christian has nothing. Every Christian has something, not only for himself but as a contribution to the general Christian atmosphere. The sanctuary of God has doorkeepers as well as prophets, congregational singing as well as solos, harps as well as trumpets. No member of the body of Christ is ever justified in issuing a declaration of independence from other Christians. Any high-hat attitude in a Christian is likely to bring one face to face with a converted bum full of the Holy Ghost used of Christ in saving souls, designed to teach "the great one" the necessity of walking humbly with God.

Variety of function creates the special temptation of Christian people. One gift comes to be more highly regarded than others and more highly regarded by some than by others. It is so easy to forget that all is of grace in the Christian life and to regard some specially gifted Christian as personal creator of his endowment. A preacher is congratulated on a sermon, a singer on a solo, a donor on his generosity, a leader on his administrative talent and so on. Presently, the hunger for praise and recognition grows and what is done is now done to be seen and heard and praised of men. So it was in the church at Corinth. Here was a church with strong deep tides of rushing spiritual life. But in time it was full of factions, divisions, schisms. They could not work and get along as they used to because there were cliques and parties in the church. The emphasis was transferred from God and Christ and the Holy Spirit to the shoulders of the gifted, and the rank and file got to feel that they did not amount to much. A sorry state for a church in primitive apostolic times! Variety of function among the members of the body of Christ caused this perversion. If those Christians had only kept their minds on Christ their living Head and on themselves as members of His body and as such charged with variety of function with no subtraction from equality of value!

A Christian is without excuse today if he forgets the full import of himself as a member of the body of Christ. The idea of variety of function must never militate against the equally basic idea of equality of value. Eye, ear, nose and throat and all the rest of the organs of the body have allotted place and function. Not one of them is warranted in saying to any of the others, "I have no need of thee." God knew what He was doing when He formed the human body. It is a unity with variety of members performing variety of functions, but from the standpoint of the body all the members of it have equal honor. Who thinks of berating any of his organs? Who contemplates anarchy and mutiny among the members of his body?

Christians have equal honor with Christ. Not talents but faithfulness is the standard of judgment. Only refusal to function is a liability. To serve the present age, Christians must give their relation to Christ priority in thought, word and deed. Only so can they be to one another what they ought to be. That Christians are necessary to one another can only be true because of what they are to Christ and because of Christ's use of them. It is Christ in a Christian which gives him his function and value in the Christian Church. It is only as Christ is given preeminence that the Christian Church and Christians individually function as the body of Christ. If the idea of the Christian Church as the body of Christ and of individual Christians as severally members of the body becomes increasingly a dynamic, operative realization in the

Church and among Christians, there will be no lack of Christian unity, no shortage of powerful influence in our modern world, but progressive, mounting service to the new world now in the making.

# XXI

## A Thematic Narrative Sermon

### Good News for Sinners
### LUKE 15:11-36

W HAT can a person do when he has wrecked his life by self-willed behaviour? Can he begin all over again as if nothing had happened? When a man's life tumbles in and lies in fragments at his feet by his own responsible action, is that all there is to it? Has a person no other recourse than to say, "Well, that's that and that finishes me"? Jesus told a parable which bears on such a situation. We know it as the parable of the Prodigal Son. It teaches that God's fellowship with man in love is broken by sin, but restored by God's forgiving love to those who truly repent. It seems to say and to keep saying: "God forgives the penitent, no matter how bad they were." It is as if Jesus wanted everybody to remember the good news of that fact and to lay it up as a sort of a theme-song: "God forgives the penitent, no matter how bad they were." The story as Jesus told it shows one who needed forgiveness above all things, who decided to make the very next move of his life a quest for forgiveness and who then experienced forgiveness as a free gift of God's love. The story may be retold for our profit in terms of these ideas: The Need of Forgiveness, The Quest of Forgiveness and the Experience of Forgiveness. The young man in Jesus' parable had to do with his father but it is clear that the father is God and the son is man the sinner, man the rebel. We propose to tell Jesus' story in fuller detail, using the lines of thought suggested for the purpose of writing it across the heavens and in every heart, that "God forgives the penitent, no matter how bad they were."

202

First, consider the Need of Forgiveness. Every person who has by his own act broken off relations with God in order to be on his own and go on his own is guilty of an enormous sin and has no greater need than the need of forgiveness. Jesus shows us a home where there are two sons. It must have been quite a home because we learn later in the story that the father had many hired servants. The father may have been a big-scale farmer or a cattle-owner and raiser who required a lot of hired help to manage his business. One first impression is that the boys in that family had about all that heart can wish. One senses a set-up which ought to be very favorable to a good and happy life.

The younger of the two sons is represented as dissatisfied. While he had all the makings of a useful and happy life right in his hand, he became bored with everything. Nothing seemed to please him. He wanted to get away to see the world. He wanted to drain the cup of life somewhere else. He knew he had no just cause for complaint. He could see that his father and mother put themselves out to be kind to him and to make everything pleasant.

He developed the habit of finding fault with everything and was often in sullen mood. His parents talked it over in private and wondered what had gotten into him. Now and again there was a scene. It may have been over some place he did not want to go to or something he did not want to do. Nothing seemed to suit. He could be very sarcastic and say things that hurt. His mother was more and more moved to tears and then his father felt it necessary to speak sharply to him.

His parents tried ever so often to reason with him. They recited to him the inventory of his blessings, naming reason upon reason why he ought to be very grateful. But it had to come out at last. He was sick and tired of his home, of his community and of about everything in his environment. He wanted to get going, to be off to see the world, to explore life's possibilities, to get away from his mother's apron strings and to be independent. When he said that last thing, his father thought he had him. He expostulated with him with pointed questions. How could the lad hope to be independent when he wanted to sever his connection with home and kindred? Ah, but it was only home and kindred he was wanting to leave. He did not intend to turn his back upon his parents' estate. He had no use for home and parents but he wanted to stuff his pockets with all their money he could carry. He would be getting a snug sum in the course of time. If his father will give it now, the son promises to trouble them no more, swearing in his heart that if he once got away with his share of the family wealth he would darken their doors no more. Modern prodigals may run off and be done with it, but the prodigal of Jesus' story is in for all he can get before he breaks away.

The father and mother had long talks when the young man was out. Father would say that he was not going to put up with it much longer and mother confessed how unhappy she was, how she was breaking under the strain and how she found it harder to carry on when all she did was unappreciated, no matter how hard she tried. So in time the decision was made to give the son what he wanted and to let him go. It was a heart-rending decision, but no other course would be possible. You cannot keep on fighting a young man's desires and embittering the home-life so that relations are in a state of tension forever. When a growing young man or woman is determined on self-willed behaviour, smashing down continually on the voice of experience, the only alternative at last is to let them have their way, to let them have their way lovingly, however reluctantly, agreeing to let them make the experiment, never ceasing to pray that goodness and mercy may follow them all the days of their lives.

When the young man's nagging persisted, the decision was made. Again, as often before, the young man said, "Give me the portion of thy substance that falleth to me." "Let me have what is coming to me. If you do that I will be off and trouble you no more." This time the father made answer while mother buried her weeping face in her apron. "Son, your mother and I have decided to do as you ask. We think you are making a mistake, but things cannot go on as they are going. I have gotten your share of the estate in portable form and here it is. If you want to leave, you may go. It will be a great sorrow to your mother and me, but you may go and we wish you well." The young man could hardly restrain himself for joy. In a few days he was off. Father went to the crest of yonder hill with him, but mother was too broken-hearted to leave her room. She did her best to control herself at the moment of parting but when he was out of sight and hearing, the cry of Rachel weeping for her children had nothing on that mother's agonized sobs and cries. At last he was off, the vile, scurrilous ingrate, who had broken his mother's heart and wrecked his loving father's happiness for well-nigh some years. His elder brother, deeply resentful of the way his parents had been treated and his brother's exasperating conduct over a prolonged period, was not like his parents praying for his welfare, but hoping to God that this brat of a brother would get what was coming to him for his own good.

That prodigal son is a figure of man in his relation to God. God gives man capacity, opportunity and responsibility. Man casts responsibility to the winds, craving opportunity to waste capacity in irresponsible, illicit pleasures. So the prodigal. So man generally. The prodigal son got everything he had together and went into a far country "and there he wasted his substance in riotous living." He put everything he had into gratifying selfish desire. There was only one person he ever thought of and that was himself. He never thought of his higher nature or his eternal interests or his God or his sins. He thought of his lusts and bent the totality of things to a life of self-gratification. Surely that boy needed forgiveness but what did he care either about his sins or their forgiveness. What does man care about God or his sins or his base ingratitude? The story goes on.

Consider, secondly, the quest for forgiveness. Things happen which cause the quest for forgiveness to be the next best thing to do, in fact, the only possible thing to do under the circumstances. The prodigal discovered the high cost of low living and that the friends you make in the far country of sin are all fair weather friends who stick to you as long as your money holds out. Periods of economic stress mark the history of man, times of scarcity and actual famine. The time came when the prodigal spendthrift had spent all and wasted all. He began to be in want. The channels between himself and others continued open only so long as he had money to shoot out. When his last cent was spent, there were no more open operating channels of social communication; but only cold, blind stares and stone barriers.

A man has to live but what can a man do who has made a hog of himself and run out of swill. He might be able to take care of swine, seeing there was such an affinity between swine and himself. He got the job but there was nothing in it like he was used to. "And he would fain have filled his belly with the husks that the swine did eat: and no man gave unto him." When a man has made his belly his god, there is nothing like an empty stomach to bring him to himself. God has strange techniques for bringing people to themselves. Here he is, the young man who got sick of his home, who had the nerve to find fault with his mother's fine cooking, who just could not stand staying in the place where he was brought up! Here he is, the young man who took his father and his mother for a ride, shot them, as it were, out of his life, taking care to load himself down with their hard-earned cash! Here he is, for whom nothing was good enough back at home, who found fault with and cursed everybody in sight, who went forth to live like a swine and at last became the companion of swine! He has come to himself. His pocket-book is empty, his stomach is empty, his soul is empty, his life is empty. He has struck bottom. There is only himself and his poverty of everything.

There is more. God has not forsaken him. There is consciousness of his condition. There is more than that. There is a new appreciation of home, of father, of mother, of all that he once despised and left. He sees himself in a new light. He sees that he has been a fool, an ingrate, a scoundrel, a miserable good-for-nothing sinner. He knows he has no right to anything. But he would like to tell his father and mother how sorry he is, what a colossal wrong he has done them. He will offer to make any possible amends by working as a hired servant. He can see that he deserves no place at his father's table. He is prepared to sleep in the barn but he simply must go to make things as right as far as true repentance can make them.

He keeps doting on what he had left when he left home, on how well it was even with his father's hired servants back on the old farm. He must go back. He must face everything. He must make a clean breast of the whole business. "I will arise and go to my father." He is even now repenting in sackcloth and ashes. He will make suitable confession and offer to make restitution by menial toil in so far as this is possible. He must perforce go empty-handed but he is sure it will not be empty-hearted. He carries a heavy burden of sorrow for his sin. He will pour that out, word for word, tear after tear, sob after sob, so that his father and mother may know that he is not the ingrate he once was but has learned a love and reverence he never knew in his apostate past. And so he sets off for home. He is on his way. He hopes to earn his way back into his father's and mother's heart.

Life gets to such a point when a man barters his fellowship with God for the pleasures of sin. When he comes to himself, he sees how he has missed it, how he has lost out, how he is all but sunk. But the love of God has always trailed him and moved him to genuine penitence. As he sits in the place he has made for himself, wan and woebegone, he realizes that he must get back to God. He will go back, face what there is to face, take what there is to take in the way of punishment, yet hoping that penitence, confession and proffered possible restitution will restore the fellowship broken by his own determined action. What will be the issue?

Consider, the experience of forgiveness. What he hoped in time to earn and pay for became the returning prodigal's experience as a gift of fatherly love. He went back as he had vowed but when he was still a long way from home, his father saw him and the meeting was a reconciliation then and there as far as the father was concerned. The embrace and the kiss of forgiveness were spontaneously given by the forgiving love of a father's heart. The son started, however, with planned but genuine confession. His repentant soul poured out itself in proper acknowledgment, "Father, I have sinned against heaven, and in thy sight: I am no more worthy to be called thy son." It is well that this came from the son. It is not hard to believe that he also said, "Make me as one of thy hired servants." It is in keeping with all the moral proprieties that the penitent prodigal should let his father know just what it was in him to confess and offer. His change of heart must be spoken.

The father is not one whit behind the son in being true to character. His loving heart is pouring itself out just as rapidly as the son's. The father is speaking to the servants, "Bring forth quickly the best robe, and put it on him; and put a ring on his hand, and shoes on his feet: and bring the fatted calf and kill it, and let us eat and make merry: for this my son was dead and is alive again; he was lost and is found." Why talk about wasted years when a brand has been snatched from the burning? No one can doubt the genuineness of the son's repentance. Use the strongest names you can think of when you describe him as he was when he blasted the lives of his parents. But square your language with the new reality. The returning prodigal is a true penitent. He repudiates every bad thing he ever did. But, of course, his experience of forgiveness is his father's gift. He did not earn it. He could not pay for it. He got it out of pure grace.

"God forgives the penitent, no matter how bad they were." God loves them. God loves the sinner right through his sin into true repentance and confession. The preacher-singer sang, "O love that will not let me go." God loves with a love that will not let a sinner go. God is forever on the trail of the sinner. Our Lord Jesus Christ, Who told the story of the prodigal, is the Good Shepherd Who came from heaven to earth, seeking to save. If conscience protests against the course you have taken, if frustration crowns your every effort to live without Christ, if striving to realize the promise of life by your own unaided powers has proved abortive, if without Christ you are more and more coming to see less and less meaning in life, if you are conscious of heading for futility and despair, we can say to you in the words of a hymn, "Lost one, 'tis Jesus, seeking to save."

God gave capacity, opportunity, responsibility. If these priceless gifts have been used to engulf life in famine and failure, God offers bread from heaven, and water of life to thirsty souls. Repent and believe the Gospel: "Believe on the Lord Jesus Christ and thou shalt be saved." God's forgiving love meets the penitent sinner while he is yet far off. Head for home. Come to Christ. "Jesus saves! Jesus saves!"

## DATE DUE

| | | | |
|---|---|---|---|
| OC. 9 '69 | | | |
| SEP 30 70 | | | |
| JL 23 71 | | | |
| FEB 16 '73 | | | |
| F | | | |
| SEP 21 '76 | | | |
| | | | |
| | | | |
| | | | |
| | | | |
| | | | |
| | | | |
| | | | |
| | | | |
| | | | |
| | | | |